SPORTONOMIC$

SPORTO

First published in 2013 by

Carlton Books
Carlton Publishing Group
20 Mortimer Street
London W1T 3JW

Text copyright © Gavin Newsham 2013

Design copyright © Carlton Books Limited 2013

A CIP catalogue for this book is available from the British Library.

ISBN 978-1-78097-265-7

Printed and bound in Great Britain by CPI Group (UK) Ltd, Croydon CR0 4YY

NOMIC$

Gavin Newsham

CARLTON

CONTENTS

INTRODUCTION

"Statistics are like bikinis – they show a lot, but not everything."

Former Major League Baseball outfielder
and manager Lou Piniella

The idea for this book began with a far-fetched thought I had about playing international football. It was November 1993 and Graham Taylor's England had just gone a goal behind to San Marino (officially the world's worst football team) after just 8.3 seconds. Though England eventually ran out 7-1 winners, the following day's newspapers were all about the Sammarinese goal-scorer, a young computer salesman by the name of Davide Gualtieri, and how this rag-tag assembly of part-time players, who had day jobs as bank clerks, plumbers and postmen, had humiliated one of international football's biggest teams.

And it got me thinking. At 22 Gualtieri was roughly the same age as myself, but unlike me he had the good fortune to be born in a small country, with an even smaller population and, most importantly, an international football side that badly needed half-decent players. This, of course, meant that the odds of him leaving behind his day job, pulling on the boots and playing against some of the biggest names in international football would always be infinitely greater than mine. I'm not saying I was ever good enough to play international football – I wasn't – but even a decent Sunday League player in the UK will never get the opportunity to take on Stuart Pearce or embarrass David Seaman, as Gualtieri did. Perhaps the local park against a pub side? Yes. But against England? Not ever.

From that day on I've been fascinated by those intriguing statistical quirks or sporting coincidences that either make you stand up and take notice, or sit back and wonder. Did you know, for example, that you've got more chance of being killed in a road accident than of making a hole-in-one at golf? Or that Scotland has the same chance of winning the 2015 Cricket World Cup as U2 frontman Bono has of becoming the next Pope?

But it goes way beyond mere probability. There are, after all, some important questions that must be addressed, questions that could, theoretically, have some catastrophic consequences. Can you really give 110 per cent without death being the inevitable outcome, for instance? Should Yorkshire seek independence from the rest of the United Kingdom? And can listening to David Bowie be the difference between winning and losing? We'll get to that later, but for now it's those nuggets of information that stick in your brain like a Justin Bieber song (without sending you over the edge) that have really prompted and inspired this book. It's the idea that you can take what appears to be a straightforward and apparently innocuous fact, and then dig a little deeper to see how things may develop should that model be applied across all sports.

It's a book that takes an alternative view of events and casts doubt on commonly accepted sporting 'facts'.

Yes, this is a book that explores the serious and the sinister, the fun and the fanciful. It's a book that takes an alternative view of events and casts doubt on commonly accepted sporting 'facts'. And it's a book that's unashamedly left field and in parts more than a little... well, weird. So if you've ever wondered what it would be like to run a Formula 1 car as a family runaround, or what might happen if everybody decided to adopt the diet of a sumo wrestler (apart from the obvious), then this is the book for you. If you haven't, then sorry, but bear with me – you won't be disappointed.

And before you say it, yes, I do need to get out more...

SPORTONOMIC$

1. HOW YOU CAN PLAY INTERNATIONAL FOOTBALL...
How your nationality can improve your chances of taking on Cristiano Ronaldo

From Albania to Zimbabwe, playing football for one's home country remains the dream of boys and men the world over. For the most part, though, such dreams will never be fulfilled, quashed cruelly by lack of talent or opportunity. There is, however, another way to make the grade in international football and it's a route not entirely dependent on an individual's ability. No, by pinpointing the right country to play for (naturalization legislation permitting), you can maximise your chances of an international cap.

The problem is two-fold, however. First, you need to adopt a FIFA-accredited nation that competes in major qualifying competitions and, second, that country must have a population small enough to provide a genuine chance of making the international squad, the idea being that when faced with a significantly smaller pool of talent to choose from, you could, theoretically, find yourself lining up against a Frank Lampard or a Leo Messi.

Of the 209 nations that make up the FIFA/Coca-Cola World Rankings[1], it's the world's oldest constitutional republic – San Marino – that vies with Bhutan and the Turks and Caicos Islands for the title of the world's worst international side.[2] A relative newcomer to international competition (their first competitive game was played in 1990), the Sammarinese have won just one match in their short history: a narrow 1-0 win over the comparative might of Liechtenstein (population: 36,010) in April 2004.[3] If you play for San Marino then, you neither expect, nor are you expected, to achieve anything of note on the field of play. That's a good thing, though – especially if you are of modest talent and currently live in one of the world's most populous countries.

In 2011 there were just 31,817 people living in the nine *castelli* that make up San Marino.[4] Of these, some 15,343 were men[5], the average age being 41.7 years.[6] If we assume that the 16–35 age group represents the ideal range from which the San Marino Football Federation select their national squad, we find that some 5,431 (35.4 per cent) of the San Marino male population falls within that group.[7] Contrast that with, say, England, where you will be competing with nearly 7 million men in the same bracket[8] and already your chances of an international cap are significantly higher, and this before we discount those who have no interest in the game or sufficient talent to play at a standard that wins recognition. But it's not purely an age thing. No, picking the right position is key to a call-up and where the greatest opportunity lies.

...picking the right position is key to a call-up and where the greatest opportunity lies.

Although there is no limit to the number of goalkeepers a country can pick for their squads, an international manager will typically pick three, meaning that at any one time there will only ever be approximately 627 goalkeepers in the international game.[9] Now of the 9,000 boys selected to attend the academies of FA Premier League and Football League clubs in 2010[10], just 9 per cent[11] went on to play first-team football, with the vast majority (78 per cent)[12] failing to become professional footballers. Moreover, in 2011 Tottenham Hotspur signed just 10 schoolboys on professional contracts from their 67-strong academy[13], the selection pool drawn from a catchment area running from Bedford and Buckinghamshire through north and south London around to Essex. In theory that's 10 players from a group of over 6 million – which for the record is about the same chance as being hit by a bus when you leave the house.[14] Crucially, of those just one was a goalkeeper.

Apply that model to San Marino and assuming fine goalkeepers are extremely rare wherever you go, of the 5,431 men available for selection in San Marino, just 489 would be good enough to be considered for the squad, with just 7.29 (or one in 67) of sufficient standard to play in goal. With the standard three goalkeepers picked for their international squad, this reduces the odds still further to just one in 2.4. Indeed, it makes an international call-up almost inevitable.

With the San Marino squad picked from the Girone A and Girone B of the 15-team Campionato Sammarinese – "it's Sunday League football by any other name"[15] – just 41 goalkeepers (i.e. the number of registered goalkeepers in the league) are theoretically competing for the three places in the international squad. To put that in perspective, it means your place in the side is statistically as likely to happen as three-time Green Jacket winner Phil Mickelson winning the 2013 Masters at Augusta or only marginally less likely than Sir Bradley Wiggins defending his Tour de France title this year.[16]

Talent aside, the problem is how one actually achieves citizenship in San Marino. If you're lucky enough to be born there or if your parents are San Marino citizens, you'll go to the front of the queue, but if you happen to be a foreign national looking to obtain citizenship, it's a more long-winded affair – not least because you must have renounced any other citizenship *and* maintained continuous residence in the Republic for at least 30 years. Clearly that makes a call-up unlikely, even if you took up residence at 18 years old. The key is to play the longer game. In taking up residence in San Marino at the earliest opportunity you might miss out on that international cap yourself, but you will give your children the greatest possible chance to play international football because citizenship obtained by naturalisation can also be passed on to resident naturalised children.[17]

NOTES & SOURCES

1. *www.fifa.com/worldrankings, January 2012.*
2. *San Marino was adopted as a constitutional republic on October 8, 1600 (www.sanmarinonline.com).*
3. *The goal-scorer was Andy Selva, San Marino's highest-ever scorer with eight goals. The next highest scorer has just two.*
4. Central Intelligence Agency (CIA) Demographic Factbook, *2011.*
5. *Ibid.*
6. *Ibid.*
7. *Ibid.*
8. *Office for National Statistics (www.statistics.gov.uk).*
9. *209 FIFA-accredited nations multiplied by three goalkeepers per international squad.*
10. *www.telegraph.co.uk/sport/football/4938593/Football-academies-kicking-and-screaming.html.*
11. *Ibid.*
12. *Ibid.*
13. *Ibid.*
14. Road Traffic Accident Survey, *Department of Transport, 2011.*
15. *Steven Archer, an Englishman playing for S.S. Murata in the Girone A, 2010.*
16. *www.paddypower.com, December 2012.*
17. *San Marino Law, November 30, 2000 n.114 'Law of citizenship' signed by Captains Regent Gian Franco Terenzi and Enzo Colombini; also by the State Secretary of Foreign Affairs, Francesca Michelotti.*

2. JOGGING ON
What if you wanted to run marathons like Haile Gebrselassie?

Haile Gebrselassie was born to run. As a child growing up in the hills of Asella, some 100 miles (160 kilometers) south of the Ethiopian capital, Addis Ababa, he used to run the six miles (9.6 km) to school every morning and another six miles on the way home in his bare feet. Then when the rainy season arrived and the shortcut across the riverbed was cut off by water, the trip to school became seven and a half miles (12 km). He was just six years old.

Two years later, Gebrselassie won his first competitive race and a new star in the world of athletics flickered into life. Later, at 15 years old, he attended an athletics meeting in Addis Ababa, intent on running the 10,000m. To his dismay, though, the race was cancelled at short notice and the only event left for him to compete in was the marathon. Undeterred, the young Gebrselassie took his place in the field and duly completed the race – his first ever marathon – in a time of just two hours and 48 minutes.

Three decades or so later and Gebrselassie's quickest time over the 26 and 385 yards (42 km) of the marathon is now a fraction under two hours and 4 minutes. He has moreover gone on to establish himself as one of, if not *the* greatest distance runner of all time. But to suggest that Gebrselassie's success is all down to genetics or his humble upbringing in rural Ethiopia is to underestimate the extent of his tenacious work ethic. After all, his is a training regime that defies belief and, quite often, nature itself. And it is one that would leave the average runner not just out of breath, but out of pocket too.

Typically, amateur marathon runners are advised to gradually increase the number of miles they run each week as their debut race approaches. Novice runners should initially aim to run 5–6 miles (8–9.6 km) three to four times a week, and then factor in a longer run at the weekends of up to 12 miles (19.3 km). As the marathon draws closer these mileages should increase, but the average total needn't exceed 40 miles (64.3 km) in order for the runner to complete the race.[1]

Gebrselassie's training regime is a little different. Rising at 6 am, he has 13 training sessions each week, with two a day from Monday to Saturday, and just the one on Sunday. He runs around 20 miles (32 kilometres) a day – *every* day – at 3 minutes 45 seconds per kilometre, a pace that is slower than his normal competition marathon pace of just under three minutes per kilometre.[2] For the amateur runner, then, this would mean that they would need to conduct

Gebrselassie runs 20 miles (32 kilometres) a day – *every* day – at 3 minutes 45 seconds per kilometre.

their training runs at 1.25 times the pace of the average London Marathon time of four hours and 20 minutes[3], making that 32km (20 miles) run take around four hours, each and every day.

But while the demands on your time will be significant, so too will those on your wallet, not least because the very nature of the training regime restricts your ability to work and therefore earn money. Gebrselassie, of course, doesn't need to worry about money, given that he commands an appearance fee of up to £250,000 ($400,000) each time he lines up in a marathon.[4] As an amateur runner, though, you won't receive anything for running, apart from encouragement.

Having the requisite wherewithal makes Gebrselassie's training regime and his daily life much more manageable. He is able to spend a significant part of his training at altitude, often at heights of 10,000 feet (3,000 metres) above sea level on a plateau overlooking his home city of Addis Ababa. Given the highest point in the United Kingdom is Ben Nevis in Scotland

(4,409 feet [1,344 metres] above sea level), this, then, will also entail some expensive foreign travel for the amateur runner if he wishes to truly replicate the Ethiopian.[5]

Having generous sponsors with deep pockets also makes Gebrselassie's life easier. His deal with sportswear manufacturer adidas, for instance, ensures that he never wants for clothing or footwear, most of which is designed to his specific requirements. Conversely, your own equipment will prove to be a significant expense, assuming, of course, you do not have a sponsorship deal in place. Running experts recommend that you change your shoes after every 400 miles (644 kilometres) of running, meaning you will have to buy a new pair of running shoes every three weeks. You will also need to replace your competition shoes after every two marathons, or every 52.4 miles (84 kilometres), as Gebrselassie does. His shoe of choice, for example, is the adidas adiZero Adios trainer and those were the shoes he wore when he set the world record for the marathon in Berlin in 2008, a race in which he bettered his own World Best by an astonishing 27 seconds. Given that the adidas adiZero Adios retails for around £85 ($136) per pair[6], you can expect to spend close to £1,500 ($2,400) every year on new running shoes.

At 5' 5" (1.65 metres) and 123lb (56 kilograms), Gebrselassie's Body Mass Index (BMI) is, at 20.47, on the lower side of a healthy weight. The average BMI of a man in the UK, meanwhile, is 26.6, and the average UK woman's BMI is 26.9, which means it's likely that you will also need to lose weight to reach Gebrselassie's BMI level.[7] The good news is that in doing as many miles each week as Haile, you will inevitably shed some of the pounds. The bad news is that his diet is so limited that it may make you wonder whether it's actually worth it. As Gebrselassie admits, he eats only because he has to and his daily intake of grain, fruit, vegetables and lean meat is designed to keep his virtually fat-free body in the peak of condition. On race days he will eat a small portion of bread and jam with tea, two hours before the race starts.[8] Like Gebrselassie, you will also need a daily massage at the end of your training.[9] In the UK, the average cost of these is around £35 ($56) per one-hour session[10], which means a total annual cost of £12,740 ($20,511).

You will then be ready for bed... at 9.30 pm.

NOTES & SOURCES

1. *www.runnersgoal.com.*
2. *www.runnersworld.com.*
3. *www.virginlondonmarathon.com.*
4. The New York Times, *November 7, 2010.*
5. The Telegraph, *March 17, 2011.*
6. *www.runnersworld.co.uk.*
7. The Lancet, *February 4, 2011.*
8. *www.therunnersguide.com.*
9. *news.bbc.co.uk/sportacademy.*
10. *The Sports Massage Association (www.thesma.org).*

3. STRONGER, FASTER, OLDER
Why the path to sporting stardom is mapped out from the day you were born

What a difference a day makes. Twenty-four little hours that can theoretically scupper your child's chances of sporting superstardom. One small day is all that it takes. It's the difference between being the biggest and best in the class or the smallest and most insignificant; the difference between being the first name on the team sheet, or the last one to be picked. It is what sports scientists call the 'Relative Age Effect'[1] and it's the very concept that can do for your kid's dreams. So why is this? Well, it's all down to something as apparently innocuous as the start of the school year.

In England, that crucial 24 hours is the difference between being born on August 31 or the following day, September 1. Yes, slip out in September and your chances of becoming a professional sports star are significantly higher than if you emerged in August, and it's all because you'll invariably be bigger and stronger than your peers.

The disparity can be significant. Take a boy born on September 1 and compare him to one born on August 31. While the two may be in the same academic year at school, there's an entire year's difference in their physical and mental development. At age 10, for instance, the difference in height between them could be anything up to 12 in (30 cm), while the variation in weight might be as pronounced as 15 lb (7 kg). In short, you know which one you want on your team.

It's easy to see why this happens, though. As coaches strive for success, the tendency to select players or athletes who are stronger, faster and more athletic means those summer-born youngsters who perhaps lack the physical prowess of their older classmates are often overlooked and with little opportunity to play, soon become disheartened and, not surprisingly, choose to do less sport. The chosen ones, or at least those perceived to have greater coordination, speed, size and talent, then receive disproportionately higher amounts of training, game play and encouragement.

But it's a problem that starts at a young age and simply persists. According to the Football Association, for instance, some 57 per cent of teenagers at English Premier League academies were born between September and December, while just 14 per cent celebrated their birthday between May and August.[2] And while the age selection dates for UEFA competitions and the rest of European club football differs – they run from January to December, not September to August – the results are even more pronounced. At the UEFA Under-17 European Championship of 2011, held in Serbia, nearly 75 per cent of the participants were born between January and April, with Christmas-born players conspicuous by their absence.[3]

From school to full international level, the evidence is fairly convincing. In the England football team that lost against Italy in the quarter-final of Euro 2012 at Kiev's Olympic Stadium on June 24, 2012, there were just three summer-born players in the starting line-up: Ashley Young (July) and Glen Johnson and Joleon Lescott (both August). Of course, that may just be some statistical quirk... then again it may not. Take England's greatest-ever team – the side that won the World Cup in 1966 – and we find only the Liverpool striker Roger Hunt was born in July, with none of that fabled side born in June or August.

But then again, take any popular team sport and invariably you'll find that the most successful participants are those born earlier in their academic years. In Australia, where the school year begins in January and ends in December, there are 33 per cent more professional players in the Australian Football League than expected with birthdays in January, and some 25 per cent fewer in December.[4] Indeed, the AFL have even discussed changing the registration dates of Australian Rules from January 1 to July 1, the idea being that by switching the dates not only do you give more youngsters an opportunity to shine, but you also perhaps tap in to a new source of talent that might otherwise have gone unnoticed, or worse still, might have been ignored. And in the National Hockey League, an organisation that has long been aware of the deleterious effects of the 'Relative Age Effect', there seems to be no fast fix for a problem that still sees over 40 per cent of their players born in the first quarter of the year, 30 per cent in the second, 20 per cent in the third and less than 10 per cent arriving in the final quarter.[5]

Even in those individual sports where you might assume that size is not so relevant as in team sports, the trend appears to continue. A study into junior fencing by the South West Talent Development Centre (a joint initiative between the University of Bath and Sport England) of July 2009 showed that of the five young female fencers recruited to the Centre that year,

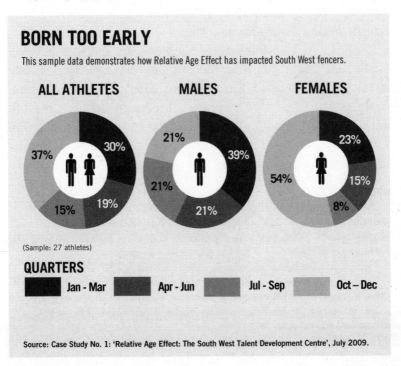

BORN TOO EARLY

This sample data demonstrates how Relative Age Effect has impacted South West fencers.

ALL ATHLETES — 37%, 30%, 15%, 19%

MALES — 21%, 39%, 21%, 21%

FEMALES — 23%, 15%, 8%, 54%

(Sample: 27 athletes)

QUARTERS
Jan - Mar | Apr - Jun | Jul - Sep | Oct – Dec

Source: Case Study No. 1: 'Relative Age Effect: The South West Talent Development Centre', July 2009.

four were born in the fourth quarter (October–December) and would therefore have been more physically developed when first introduced to the sport at primary school – and this despite the best fencers not reaching their peak until their mid-twenties.[6]

Clearly, it's a trend mirrored around the world, irrespective of the sport, and one that can crush the hopes of the wide-eyed youngster with a dream and his eyes on the big time. And therein lies the problem. You see, unless your child is abundantly talented (or abnormally well-built for their age), they will never get noticed, let alone picked. It is, in effect, an *un*-level playing field.

NOTES & SOURCES

1. *'Definition: The Relative Age Effect or Effects (RAE)'* describes the biased situation that favours older children in each age group due to their superior physical, emotional and psychological development relative to their younger peers.

2. The Football Association, National Academies Directory.

3. Figures supplied by Andy Roxburgh, technical director, UEFA.

4. *'Analysing Seasonal Health Data'*, Dr Adrian Barnett and Professor Annette Dobson, University of Queensland, February 2010.

5. Journal of the Canadian Association for Health, *'Physical Education, and Recreation'*, Nov–Dec, 23–28.

6. *Case Study No. 1: 'Relative Age Effect: The South West Talent Development Centre'*, July 2009.

4. THE NAMING GAME
What's in a name? Quite a lot if it's your team that's selling it...

In this modern era, the world of sport and the demands of business are inextricably linked. Sponsors and partners dominate major events such as the Olympic Games and the FIFA World Cup Finals. Trophies and tournaments are regularly re-badged, and players bound by long-term, multi-million commercial contracts that bring them untold riches, all for wearing a particular boot, shirt or even watch.

Today there is virtually no area or aspect of sport that hasn't got a price, and the concept of 'naming rights' is as much part of the industry as any other. But while selling the rights to, say, a team shirt is a lucrative and fairly unobtrusive way to raise revenues for your club, the idea that a team could sell the name of its own stadium is, while commonplace in the US, still something of a thorny issue in the UK. Never was this more evident than at Newcastle United, where in 2011 the club's owner Mike Ashley announced that the name of their home ground since 1892, St James' Park, would now change to become the Sports Direct Arena. While the name change itself would not bring in any additional revenue – Sports Direct is one of Ashley's companies – this was a move designed purely to attract other investors into taking over the name of the Magpies' treasured home ground.

Yet the furore that greeted Ashley's decision to change the name of St James' Park was a clear indication of how fans, in the UK at least, hold certain things very dear. Increasingly, though, it's happening right across British football and even though they might resent it, the fans are powerless to prevent this from happening. Hallowed and much-loved grounds like Bolton

Wanderers' Burnden Park, Brighton & Hove Albion's Goldstone Ground and Arsenal's Highbury Stadium have all gone, with the clubs now respectively playing their home games in the Reebok Stadium (named after a sportswear and equipment firm), the American Express Community Stadium (credit cards) and the Emirates Stadium (a Middle Eastern airline). And while the grounds are modern, spacious and designed to give fans the best possible view of the action, you can't help but feel that a little bit of the game dies each time an old ground is razed and a new one, complete with full corporate branding (and a nondescript or vaguely comical name), replaces it.

As is often the case with corporate initiatives in sport, the trend began in the United States of America. Back in 1926, the owner of the Chicago Cubs, the chewing gum magnate William Wrigley, named the team's home ground 'Wrigley Field' and in so doing opened up a new and previously unexplored way for sports clubs and franchises to raise revenue. Since then, the naming of stadia in the US has become the norm. And who cares if that means going to watch your team in a venue that sounds more like a corporation's HQ than a sports stadium? Fancy seeing the Houston Astros baseball team in action? Then head on over to the Minute Maid Park. Want to see the Los Angeles Galaxy do their thing? Just make your way to the Home Depot Center, a stadium named after a DIY store.

So, why do they do it? Well, in the case of the Houston Astros, for example, it was the small matter of a deal worth over £62 million ($100 million), 28-year deal that convinced them to do business with the soft drinks giant. That said, the Astros were left high and dry by the bankruptcy of the ground's previous sponsor, the scandal-ridden Enron Corporation. And it's not just the top-flight teams that make the money. Even in US college sport the sums to be made from selling the name of your ground can make a huge difference to the team's future progress. For example, the University of Lousiana's deal to sell their arena name to KFC Yum! (parent company of KFC, Pizza Hut and Taco Bell) netted them £8.4 million ($13.5 million) over 10 years.[1]

Everything, it seems, is open to offers. Occasionally, entire sports clubs have their name and identity changed as a new owner comes in with new ideas as to how they want things to be. In US Major League Soccer, one of the League's original teams, the New York/New Jersey MetroStars, was taken over in 2006 and they soon found themselves with new team colours, a new club logo and even a new name – the New York Red Bulls (even though they play in New Jersey).

Nothing is exempt and increasingly clubs, teams and even individuals are employing ever more imaginative ways in which to exploit their names and profiles. As far back as 1980, when the British and New Zealand runner Nick

Nothing is exempt and increasingly clubs, teams and even individuals are employing ever more imaginative ways in which to exploit their names...

Akers changed his name by deed poll to 'Nick Vladivar' to take advantage of a sponsorship offer from Vladivar Vodka[2], there has always been a sportsman or woman who needs a little extra backing when more conventional methods of raising finance are not exactly forthcoming. In 2007, the Tonga rugby player Epi Taione accepted a "five-figure" offer from the Irish bookmaker Paddy Power to legally change his own name to 'Paddy Power' for the duration of the 2007 World Cup tournament, so long as the fee went to help fund the cash-strapped Tongan team's campaign.[3] The deal duly struck, Taione, or rather Power, went on to lead Tonga to their best-ever results in the event, although the plan for the team to dye their hair green for the tournament was called off at the very last minute.

NAME THAT GROUND...

Ten of the strangest names ever to have been sold.

DICK'S SPORTING GOODS PARK
Location: Colorado, USA
Capacity: 18,086
Team: Colorado Rapids
Sponsor: Dick's Sporting Goods, sports equipment retailer

PIZZA HUT PARK
Location: Frisco, Texas, USA
Capacity: 20,500
Team: FC Dallas
Sponsor: Pizza Hut (the deal expired in 2012)

KFC YUM! CENTER
Location: Louisville, Kentucky, USA
Capacity: 22,090
Team: Louisville Cardinals
Sponsor: Yum! (owners of KFC, Pizza Hut and Taco Bell)

FLANCARE PARK
Location: Longford, Republic of Ireland
Capacity: 6,850
Team: Longford FC
Sponsor: Flancare, warehousing and logistics (not a flan case manufacturer!)

DUNKIN' DONUTS CENTER
Location: Providence, Rhode Island, USA
Capacity: 13,106
Teams: Providence Bruins and Providence Friars
Sponsor: Dunkin' Donuts

HUNKY DORYS PARK
Location: Drogheda, Republic of Ireland
Capacity: 2,000
Team: Drogheda United FC
Sponsor: Hunky Dorys crisps and snacks

KITKAT CRESCENT
Location: York, England
Capacity: 7,872
Team: York City FC
Sponsor: Nestlé Rowntree, confectionery (the deal expired in 2010)

WHATABURGER FIELD
Location: Corpus Christi, Texas, USA
Capacity: 5,400
Team: Corpus Christi Hooks
Sponsor: Whataburger – 'home of the bigger, better burger'

CAPITAL ONE FIELD
Location: Maryland, USA
Capacity: 54,000
Team: Maryland Terrapins
Sponsor: Capital One, credit cards

BOJANGLES' COLISEUM
Location: Charlotte, North Carolina, USA
Capacity: 9,605
Teams: Carolina Speed and the Charlotte Copperheads
Sponsor: Bojangles' Famous Chicken 'n Biscuits

NOTES & SOURCES

1. *www.cbsnews.com, April 19, 2010.*
2. *www.nickakers.com.*
3. *news.bbc.co.uk/1/hi/northern_ireland/6977125.stm.*

5. OLDEST SWINGERS IN TOWN
Or why sporting life doesn't really begin at 40

Readers of a certain age will recall with fondness the story of the Ethiopian long-distance runner Miruts Yifter. The winner of the 5,000 and 10,000m gold medals at the Moscow Olympics, Yifter's astonishing finishing kick in the closing stages of his races earned him the affectionate nickname of 'Yifter the Shifter'. But it wasn't only his incredible turn of pace that had people talking back in 1980. When asked in the wake of his wins how old he was, Yifter, with his balding pate and wiry frame, was non-committal. "Men may steal my chickens, men may steal my sheep," he insisted. "But no man can steal my age!"

Reports at the time had Yifter's age at anywhere between 33 and 42, although he actually looked even older. Even the International Association of Athletics Federations couldn't decide between January 1, 1938, or May 15, 1944 as his official birthday. All everyone could agree on was that Miruts Yifter was brilliantly talented on the one hand but unusually mature for a Olympic long-distance runner.

Someone, somewhere once said that "age ain't nothing but a number", but in the world of sport it can determine just how long you'll be able to compete. Professional footballers, for instance, will often defend their high wages by arguing that theirs is a short career, and they're right as few players get to enjoy 20 years playing the game. In other sports, like, say, shooting, a competitor can carry on and on without the need to maintain supreme level of physical fitness. Mental alertness certainly, but not physical fitness; they can start at 16 and end at 60, if they like.

It all depends on the sport. Boxers, of course, are notorious for coming back for one last shot at glory and it's rare for retired champions to actually stay retired. So while the British Light Welterweight Ricky Hatton came out of retirement in late 2012 to fight again at the comparatively young age of 34, with other boxers there seems no limit to when they can still climb through the ropes. George Foreman is one of the best examples here. Having retired in 1977, 'Big George' returned to the ring in 1987 and regained the World Heavyweight Championship by knocking out Michael Moorer in 1994. At 45 he remains the oldest Heavyweight Champion in history, but he's not the oldest boxing world champion. That honour currently belongs to the American Light Heavyweight Bernard Hopkins Jr, who, aged 46 years, four months and six days, defeated Canada's Jean Pascal at Montreal's Bell Centre in May 2011 to eclipse Foreman's long-standing record.

It's the sports that require a more mental approach, like snooker and golf, where the over-40s still prosper.

While boxing is one of those sports with such a physically punishing training schedule that fighters might be forgiven for throwing in the towel as soon as time begins to take its toll, there are many sports where age is no real barrier to success. In snooker, where six-times World Champion Steve Davis still plays at a high level aged 55, there is little to stop players competing other than a lack of motivation to put the hours in on the practice table and a desire to stay at home rather than travel the world on tour. Darts is the same, and the world's greatest-ever player, Phil 'The Power' Taylor, managed to secure eight world titles in his 40s and recently won his 13th World Matchplay, aged 52.[1]

The recurring theme, then, is how those sports that do not require speed and agility, explosive power and/or endurance, can theoretically lead to a much longer sporting career. Indeed, it's those sports that require a more mental approach, like snooker, where the over-40s still prosper. It's also why more sedentary sports find favour among the older generation. Golfers, of course, can carry on playing into their dotage and it's not uncommon for Majors to be won by 40-something players. Jack Nicklaus, for example, famously won the Masters at Augusta in 1986 when he rolled back the years to win the green jacket at 46, while his rival from the 1970s and 80s, Tom Watson, very nearly created the greatest golf story of them all when he came within a par putt of securing his sixth Open Championship at Turnberry in 2009, aged almost 60.

Again, though, golf doesn't require any great physical exertion. Yes, players may walk over four miles (6.4 kilometres) during the course of a round, but they do have someone else carrying their golf bag around with them, which can weigh anything between 30–50lb (14–23 kilograms).[2] It's for that reason that even when players' careers come to an end on the regular PGA and European Tours, they can still carry on playing on the over-50s Champions and Seniors Tours, where the prize money is still significant but the living is that little bit easier.

Even at the Olympics, where the cream of the world's athletic talent convenes, there is still an a significant number of competitors who don't exactly conform to the stereotypical image of an Olympian. At London 2012, for example, there were 187 athletes competing at the Games who were over 40 years of age, including two 65-year-olds: the Latvian shooter, Afanasijs Kuzmins and the Canadian show jumper, Ian Millar.[3] Indeed, in show jumping and equestrian events more generally, there is a marked incidence of older participants, especially when compared to other sports. At London 2012, the average age of a competitor was 26, whereas the average age of an equestrian rider was 38. That, in part, was down to the participation of Japan's Hiroshi Hoketsu, who competed in the dressage event at the age of 71, some 48 years after he competed in his first Olympic Games – Tokyo, 1964.

Hoketsu's chosen sport is unique in that sense, as it's not uncommon for riders in their fifties and sixties to still compete at the highest level. Britain's Nick Skelton was 54 when he took the gold as part of the Team Jumping squad at London 2012, and has already set his sights on defending his title in Rio de Janeiro in 2016. That Skelton was still able to ride at 54 was remarkable. That he was still able to compete at the highest level – and win – was simply extraordinary, not least because he had suffered a broken neck in 2000 and had also undergone a hip replacement and two knee operations in recent years as well. Had that happened in most other sports, his career would certainly have been over.

Generally speaking, the equestrian events appear to offer both riders and jockeys comparatively long professional careers, provided they can keep their weight down. In horse racing, Lester Piggott won the 2,000 Guineas on Rodrigo de Triano at the age of 56, while his rival Willie Carson retired from racing in 1996, aged 54. A rider or jockey's longevity in the saddle, then, not only demonstrates how certain sports offer more of an opportunity to compete, irrespective of the passing of time, but also shows that when something else, be it animal or machine, is responsible for bearing the brunt of the exertion involved, it can massively extend a sportsperson's career.

It's only in those sports where physical fitness is key that the careers are understandably shorter. In games like football the evidence is easy to see, especially with outfield players whose gradual inability to keep up with the pace of play can easily be exposed. Few professional players make it past 40 and the former England striker Teddy Sheringham holds the record as the oldest outfield player to have competed in the English Premier League when he turned out for West Ham United just 93 days short of his 41st birthday.

The exception to the rule is goalkeepers, whose careers usually last well into their late 30s and often into their 40s, too. Peter Shilton, England's most capped international, won the last of his caps for his country aged 40 at the World Cup Finals in Italy of 1990 and carried on goalkeeping in the Football League until he was 47, amassing a total of 1,005 League appearances.

In terms of a World Champion in football, however, it is the legendary Italian goalkeeper Dino Zoff who takes the plaudits, having captained his country to victory in the World Cup Finals in Spain of 1982, aged 40 years, 4 months and 13 days.[4]

Of course, everyone reacts differently to the ageing process and not everybody's physiological age will tally with their chronological age. Look at Merlene Ottey; in the 2000 Olympics in Sydney, aged 40, she became the oldest female track and field medallist in history when she anchored the Jamaican Women's 4 x 100 metres relay team to a silver medal. Later, she was also awarded a bronze in the individual 100m when the USA's Marion Jones was stripped of her title for doping offences. Incredibly, Ottey, now a resident of Slovenia, is still sprinting to a very high level and in 2012, aged 52, she even anchored the Slovenian 4 x 100 metres team at the European Athletic Championships.

Incredibly, Merlene Ottey, now a resident of Slovenia, is still sprinting to a very high level, aged 52...

It's safe to assume then that the likes of Sheringham and Ottey are, or were, in a rare minority – genetic anomalies undeterred by the ageing process. For some athletes, their career length is largely determined by genes and heredity; for others, the effects of their chosen lifestyle finally take their toll. What's clear is that many of the significant changes in a person's body, be they a professional athlete or professional hairdresser, start to occur around the age of 40. According to the American Academy of Orthopaedic Surgeons, it's around this age that a person's muscles will begin to lose tissue and fibre mass, seriously decreasing the ability to respond to activity. Moreover, tendons start to lose water, reducing their effectiveness and tolerance to stress. The metabolism also slows, making weight gain more probable. Bones begin to soften, making fractures more likely to happen and less likely to heal properly. The heart, meanwhile, gradually weakens, becoming less efficient at pumping the necessary quantities of blood quickly around the body. This, in turn, makes you tire more quickly.[5]

And they say life begins at 40.

NOTES & SOURCES

1. *www.bbc.co.uk/sport/0/darts/19043124.*
2. *www.cleveland.com/golf/index.ssf/2011/08/inside_the_life_of_a_pga_caddie.html.*
3. *www.guardian.co.uk/sport/datablog/2012/aug/07/olympics-2012-athletes-age-weight-height#age.*
4. *www.fifa.com.*
5. *orthoinfo.aaos.org*

6. REGIONAL PRIDE AT THE OLYMPIC GAMES
Just who were the real stars of London 2012?

Geographical divisions have long been the source of many a pub argument, not to mention political and economic disputes and, for that matter, all-out war. In sport, of course, it is one of the key ingredients in establishing and sustaining a healthy or, as is often the case, an unhealthy relationship between two opposing participants. England versus Scotland in football, India v Pakistan in cricket, or Europe and the USA in golf's Ryder Cup; these are epic rivalries that as well as being rooted in political and social divisions, happen to be compounded by geography too. Put simply, it's so much more than mere bragging rights.

It's no different in domestic sport, where tensions run high and the mere location of a geographical feature such as a mountain range or a river can be enough for supporters to take an instant and usually irrational dislike to anyone who happens to come from the other side. Famously, for example, the very existence of the Pennines has for centuries helped foster decidedly frosty relations between the counties of Lancashire and Yorkshire, so when the London 2012 Olympic Games arrived and Yorkshire's athletes performed so creditably, it seemed as if the White Rose county finally had one up on their Lancastrian rivals.

While much was made of the performance of athletes from Yorkshire at London 2012 – it was even claimed that an independent Yorkshire would have taken 12th place on the medal table, winning as many golds as sports-mad nations like

Australia[1] – the truth, however, is that Yorkshire actually lags behind many counties in the number of Olympians it produces. Yes, while the results of the likes of Jessica Ennis and Nicola Adams, Ed Clancy and the Brownlee brothers may have suggested that the White Rose county was a hotbed of athletic talent, the evidence suggests that Yorkshire is actually a county of marked underachievement.

Prior to the 2012 Games, West Yorkshire had produced 91 Olympians since the inaugural Games took place in 1896, which is 30 per cent lower than the average for a county with the size of its population; while South Yorkshire, home to heptathlete gold medallist Ennis, had produced 60, some 21 per cent lower than average for its size. North Yorkshire, meanwhile, had produced 56 Olympians – 10 per cent lower than average for its population, whereas the East Riding of Yorkshire could only boast 17, or 51 per cent lower than average.

It's a similar story when it comes to converting these appearances into winning medals. While the results at London 2012 will have gone some way toward redressing the balance, prior to the Games, North Yorkshire had won 22 medals (5 per cent lower than average), South Yorkshire had won 17 (40 per cent lower), West Yorkshire had won 25 (48 per cent lower) and East Riding had won just five medals (61 per cent lower).

Irritatingly for those proud Yorkshiremen and women, it's their neighbours and rivals across the Pennines who seem to have a real knack of producing Olympians. In Merseyside, for example, they have produced 105 (35 per cent higher than average), while down the M62 in Greater Manchester they have had 184 to their credit (322 per cent higher). Indeed, wherever there is a major city or conurbation, there seems to be a preponderance of Olympians – due, primarily, to the greater access to facilities that urban athletes enjoy and, of course, a much higher population. Edinburgh and Glasgow have 79 per cent and 54 per cent respectively more than average numbers of Olympians, Bristol has 58 per cent higher and South Glamorgan, home to the Welsh capital Cardiff, has 57 per cent more Olympians than it should. Greater London, meanwhile, has produced 1,005 Olympians in the modern era, a staggering 124 per cent higher than it should for its population.[2]

For many, the fact that 'Team Yorkshire' did so well at London 2012 – athletes from the county won seven golds, two silvers and three bronzes – merely reinforced a long-held, if tongue-in-cheek, belief that it should break away from the UK and become an independent state. But for the likes of Scotland, the success of their athletes at the Games wasn't just one great stride toward some distant (and light-hearted) Utopia; no, for Scotland, a country in the midst of a fierce debate to determine whether it should become independent from the rest of the UK, it was, on the face of it, a boost to the Scottish National Party and those who favour a severing of ties with Whitehall. In total, Scottish athletes won 14 medals at London 2012[3], a performance that represented fifth of all the medals won by Team GB[4] and that would have given Scotland 12th place in the final medals table, were they a stand-alone nation.

Scottish athletes won 14 medals at London 2012... and that would have given Scotland 12th place in the final medals table, were they a stand-alone nation.

Yet what appeared to be a successful campaign for Scotland wasn't actually that successful at all. Why? Because 12 out of the 14 Scottish medal-winning athletes, including Andy Murray, Katherine Grainger and Britain's most successful Olympian of all time, Sir Chris Hoy, all live in England. Moreover, 11 of these were partly-funded by the UK National Lottery, while all trained at UK (not Scottish) governing body facilities and just one, the show jumper Scott Brash, actually lived in his homeland.[5] More galling for the SNP campaign, perhaps, was the sight and sound of the Olympic legend and Knight of the Realm, Sir Chris Hoy, not only riding his lap of honour draped in the Union Flag[6] but openly rejecting the idea of an independent Scotland. "I'm Scottish and I'm British, I think you can be both

– they are not mutually exclusive," he said. "All I can say is that I'm very proud to be part of this team, to be part of the British team, to be alongside English and Welsh and guys from the Isle of Man. It's been great and I'm proud to be part of it." In that respect, one of the main and most immediate effects of the Team GB gold rush was not merely the sigh emanating from SNP leader Alex Salmond, but the glorious and overwhelming affirmation of the Union.

NOTES & SOURCES

1. *Yorkshire Athletes Score 12 Medals, Press Association, August 12, 2012.*
2. *Data from OlyMadMen, Sports Reference (www.sports-reference.com).*
3. *Eight golds, four silvers and one bronze.*
4. *Great Britain won 65 medals, taking third place in the medals table behind the USA and China.*
5. *UK Sport & Team GB official records.*
6. *Chris Hoy also led Team GB out at the Opening Ceremony, carrying the Union Flag.*

7. WHY FOOTBALL'S DIVERS LEAVE FANS OUT OF POCKET
The real impact of injuries and simulation

While players, pundits and commentators of a certain age bemoan the lack of physical contact in the modern game, professional football remains a sport where injuries sustained from tackling are still commonplace. It is, after all, a contact sport. At all levels of the game, from Premier League down to pub team, the incidence of injury is higher in football than in many other sports, including basketball, cricket, badminton, cycling, judo and swimming. It's even higher than a notoriously physical game like rugby, or even one such as boxing where the sole purpose of the sport is to hurt your opponent.

A survey of the most common football injuries by PhysioRoom. com revealed that the most frequent complaint afflicting English Premier League players is a hamstring strain, followed by a sprained ankle, knee cartilage tear, hernia and injuries to the anterior cruciate ligament. The majority of injuries in the game are caused by trauma (ie colliding with another player or landing awkwardly) and occur at a rate of between nine and 35 injuries per 1,000 hours of football, with age being a significant contributory factor in the likelihood of suffering an injury.[1]

In football, then, very real injury lurks around every corner and it's not just from being the unlucky one who happens to be on the receiving end of an ugly two-footed lunge. Yes, despite massive improvements in the quality of the actual balls used in the game in the post-war period, the very fact that the player is still using parts of his body to propel them (when those body parts were not designed to carry out such tasks) does leave him open to further injury and, in some cases, long-term health problems. The cumulative effect of heading a ball, for instance, has long been thought to be a contributory factor in the degeneration of brain cells. Indeed, it was cited as a reason for the death of the former West Bromwich Albion and England player Jeff Astle, who died, aged 59, in 2002. The coroner ruled that repeatedly heading the heavy, old-style leather footballs of the 1960s and early 70s 'made at least a significant contribution to [Astle's degenerative brain] disease'.[2] However, despite the massive strides that have been made in terms of lowering the weight of the football, there is evidence to suggest that heading it can still pose a significant threat to one's health, not least because the ball itself can often travel at speeds in excess of 60mph (105kph).

Analysis suggests there's a safe cut-off point of around 1,000 headers a year – less than three headers a day.

In November 2011, the US researcher Dr Michael Lipton of Montefiore Medical Center (the university hospital for the Albert Einstein College of Medicine) published his initial findings into the damage that heading the football can cause. Using a brain scan, or diffusion tensor imaging, Lipton tested 32 amateur football players and found that those who felt that they headed the ball on a regular basis had clear and obvious signs of mild traumatic brain injury, and that five regions of the brain were damaged, most notably those areas at the front of the brain and toward the back of the skull that help aid attention, memory and some visual functions.[3]

Lipton's analysis also suggested that there was a safe cut-off point of around 1,000 headers a year, a figure below which players could not expect to suffer any damage. While that may seem like a lot of headers, for a professional player who trains virtually every day and plays twice a week, it's a very small number, amounting perhaps to less than three headers a day – a number that they probably complete in 10 or 15 minutes of training.

Superficially at least, the impact of heading a ball repeatedly would appear not dissimilar to that suffered by a boxer from receiving blows to the head on a regular basis. There have been many studies into the risk of brain damage in professional boxing, the majority of which concur on the very real risks that being a pro fighter entails, but even in amateur boxing, where the fighters wear protective headguards, the risk of brain damage is still high. A study by Max Hietala of Gothenburg's Sahlgrenska University Hospital in 2007 found that even amateur boxers have raised levels of the biochemical markers for brain injury in the cerebrospinal fluid (CSF), especially after a fight. One particular marker for brain damage, the neurofilament light (NFL), was four times higher in boxers within 10 days of a fight than in healthy non-boxers. Moreover, those boxers who had received more than 15 significant punches during their bout had seven or eight times of NFL in the post-fight period. "Repeated hits to the head are potentially damaging to the central nervous system, and our results suggest CSF-analysis could be used for medical counselling of athletes after boxing or head injury," concluded Hietala.

Interestingly, Hietala also extended his study to see if there were comparable effects on the brain from football players repeatedly heading the ball from long and high goal kicks. No increased levels of biochemical markers for brain damage in cerebrospinal fluid were found. "This data shows heading in soccer is not associated with any neurochemical evidence of brain damage," said Hietala.

That said, serious football injuries are rare and there are few so-called 'career-ending tackles' that actually end a player's career. Yes, the injuries may appear serious – and they often are – but rarely does an injured player never take to the field again. In February 2008, for example, Arsenal striker Eduardo Alves da Silva suffered a broken left fibula and an open dislocation of his left ankle after a tackle by the Birmingham City defender

Martin Taylor. It was an injury so graphic that Sky Sports, who were broadcasting the game live on television, refused to show any close-ups of the incident, while the Arsenal manager Arsène Wenger called for a lifetime ban for Taylor. To the viewer at home, it looked for all the world as if da Silva might never walk again, let alone play football, but almost a year to the day, he was back in action for Arsenal and, more recently, playing as well as ever for his new club, Shakhtar Donetsk.

While injuries like this are rare, the incidence of players actually faking or feigning injury seems to be on the increase. Diving (or 'simulation' as it's now officially known) is so rife in the professional game that one never really knows just how badly a player is injured, or if he's even injured at all.

The study by Paul Morris and David Lewis found four clear ways in which players attempt to deceive the referee, and how best they might be spotted.

The proliferation of such incidents led researchers at the University of Portsmouth to look into diving and the number of 'injuries' that happen where the referee has to stop the game to allow the player to get treatment. With diving and/or the exaggeration of the effect of a tackle, the study by Paul Morris and David Lewis found four clear ways in which players attempt to deceive the referee and how best they might be spotted.[5] The first, which accounted for 29 per cent of all examples, was what they termed 'Temporal Continuity', wherein the player leaves too much time between contact and reaction. The second most common was the 'Archer's Bow', whereby the player bends backwards and raises an arm so as to attract the referee's attention, while the third, accounting for 25 per cent, was the 'Ballistic Continuity', where there is a clear and disproportionate reaction for the level of contact made. Finally, Morris and Lewis identified what they called 'Contact Consistency', where a player gets hit in one area but acts as if it's another. A classic example of this occurred in the 2002 World Cup game between Brazil and Turkey, when the

Turkish player Hakan Ünsal kicked the ball at Brazil's Rivaldo, striking him on the legs. Rivaldo, however, collapsed on the turf, clutching his face. Ünsal, meanwhile, was sent off and Brazil went on to win the game.

The frequency of simulation like this in the matches that Morris and Lewis analysed led them to assess just what effect it was having on the game itself. Using their four criteria, they found that there was an average of 11 bogus injuries or incidents per match with only one *bona fide* injury that genuinely required treatment from the physio. While this would not really be of much consequence if the match referee actually added on the correct amount of time to make up for the stoppage, Morris and Lewis found that invariably officials would add on no more than three to four minutes of additional time when the actual figure was at least seven minutes.

All of which means, of course, that the average Premier League football match lasts just 86.5 minutes. Or does it? Well, in the 2010–11 Premier League season, the average time the ball was actually in play was just 62 minutes 39 seconds, a figure which, when you subtract the time referees fail to add on, then falls to 59 minutes and 9 seconds, or roughly two-thirds of the actual match time of 90 minutes. With the average adult match-day ticket in the Premier League now costing £48.90 ($79)[6], this means that the fans are effectively paying around £16.30 ($26) for little more than watching a ball-boy retrieve a football or a few grown men roll around on the grass when there's only an 8.33 per cent chance that they're actually hurt.

NOTES & SOURCES

1. *www.physio.room*
2. *www.telegraph.co.uk/news/uknews/1412908/Jeff-Astle-killed-by-heading-ball-coroner-rules.*
3. *www.sciencedaily.com/releases/2011/11/111129092420.*
4. *'Olympic Boxing May Damage the Brain', University of Gothenburg, April 23, 2012.*
5. *'Tackling Diving: The Perception of Deceptive Intentions in Association Football (Soccer)', Paul H. Morris and David Lewis, Journal of Nonverbal Behaviour, Vol.1, 2010.*
6. *'The Price of Football', BBC Sport website survey, August 2011.*

8. DON'T GIVE UP THE DAY JOB
Why Olympic success doesn't always save you from the nine-to-five

At the London 2012 Olympics, the sprinter Usain Bolt ran for around 100 seconds. In that time, the 26-year-old from Trelawny, Jamaica, succeeded in retaining his 100m, 200m and 4 x 100m titles, becoming the first man in history to achieve the feat. Bolt's unparalleled success on the track has not only made him the biggest star in his sport, but has also made him a very rich man.

Today, he commands an appearance fee of £218,000 ($350,000) – or around £22,789 ($36,534) per second – each time he runs in an international track meeting, although his actual pay on the track is but pin money compared to his earnings away from it. Since his junior running days in 2002, he has been sponsored by the sports clothing and equipment manufacturer, Puma; today, having signed a new deal with the company in 2010, he is paid a reported £5.6 million ($9 million) each year – the largest sponsorship deal ever awarded to a track athlete. He also enjoys lucrative deals with the likes of Gatorade, Nissan, Visa, Hublot and Virgin Media. In all, it's estimated that Bolt earned in excess of £12.5 million ($20 million) in 2012, while his total worth is expected to eclipse £62.3 million ($100 million) by the time the next Games come round in Rio de Janiero in 2016.[1]

Of course, Usain Bolt is unquestionably the number one transcendent star in the world of Olympic sport, a larger-than-life character who fills stadia and captivates television viewers in their millions. Sadly, it's not the same for every athlete who reaches the pinnacle of his or her sport, as the following table shows.

OLYMPIANS AND THEIR OCCUPATIONS

Reaching the Olympics doesn't always mean that you can quit your day job.

IBRAHIM BALLA

Country: Australia

Sport: Boxing

Occupation: Plumber

Average salary: **£43,607 (US$70,207)** [2]

URIGE BUTA

Country: Norway

Sport: Marathon

Occupation: Janitor

Average salary: **£35,776 (US$57,599)** [3]

DINA ASPANDIYAROVA

Country: Australia

Sport: Shooting

Occupation: Travel Agent

Average salary: **£37,651 (US$60,618)** [4]

GWEN JORGENSEN

Country: USA

Sport: Triathlon

Occupation: Accountant with Ernst & Young

Average salary: **£35,813 (US$57,658)** [5]

LANCE BROOKS

Country: USA

Sport: Discus throwing

Occupation: Construction worker

Average salary: **£28,274 (US$45,521)** [6]

DEBBIE CAPOZZI

Country: USA

Sport: Sailing

Occupation: She works in her family's italian ice cream shop

Average salary: **£25,759 (US$41,471)** [7]

CHI YIP CHEUNG

Country: Hong Kong

Sport: Judo

Occupation: Fireman

Average salary: **£13,980 (US$22,507)** [8]

NATASHA PERDUE

Country: Great Britain

Sport: Weightlifting

Occupation: Refuse collector

Average salary: **£19,850 (US$31,958)** [9]

NOTES & SOURCES
1. *www.therichest.org.*
2. *www.mycareer.com.au.*
3. *www.mylittlenorway.com.*
4. *www.payscale.com/research/AU.*
5. *www.glassdoor.com.*
6. *www.indeed.com.*
7. *www.glassdoor.com.*
8. *www.hkfsd.gov.hk.*
9. *www.mysalary.co.uk.*

9. RED IS THE COLOUR
Can wearing a specific colour increase your chances of sporting success?

With the riches on offer in sport spiralling ever upward, it's understandable, if not entirely acceptable, that athletes continue to seek any advantage that will give them an edge in the heat of competition. For many, it's the little things, those peculiar idiosyncrasies that can make the difference between success and failure, glory and despair. And if something works – no matter how ridiculous – then they tend to stick with it until such time as their luck takes a turn for the worse.

For many this manifests itself as a reliance or even an over-reliance on superstition. It might be a lucky pair of shorts, such as the ones Michael Jordan wore under his Chicago Bulls pair; being the last player to walk out of the tunnel (a favourite of footballer Paul Ince); or even a strict insistence on a particular diet, like the young British tennis player Heather Watson, who insisted on eggs and smoked salmon for breakfast every single day during her run to the third round of the Wimbledon Championships of 2012. Major League Baseball relief pitcher Turk Wendell, who played for the likes of the New York Mets, was so superstitious that not only would he brush his teeth between innings, but he would also wear a necklace made of the teeth of the animals he had killed while hunting.

While it is difficult to quantify the strength and comfort generated from such rituals, the quest to find legal advantages in actual competition remains intense, and even something so apparently inconsequential as the colour of the kit or uniform a player wears has been shown to be of considerable psychological, if not physical advantage.

Famously, the golfer Tiger Woods, a player who dominated the game in the late 1990s and throughout the 2000s, always chooses to wear a red shirt on the final day of a competition. It was less of a fashion statement, more one of intent. "I wear red on Sundays because my mom thinks that that's my power colour – and you know you should always listen to your mom," he explained.[1]

While Woods was right to heed his mother's advice, her assertion that red is a "power colour" has long been the subject of academic investigation, both within sport and in a wider context. At Cambridge University, for example, anthropologist Dr Joanna Setchell's studies of African monkeys suggest that it is those males with a distinct red colouration that have an advantage when it comes to mating, and that red, across all species, is the colour indicating dominance and control.[2] Even in the human world, a red face is often seen as a sign of anger and aggression, while a pale face invariably signifies fear.

In those contests where both fighters appeared to be equally matched, the number of wins for the contestant in red was significantly higher.

Certainly in the world of sport there is a wealth of evidence to reinforce the idea that the colour red maintains a strange and significant hold over the opposition, and examination of the success rate of the sports performers and teams who wear red (whether or not by choice) backs up the idea that there is a clear and distinct advantage to playing in the colour. Two researchers from the University of Durham, Russell Hill and Robert Barton, have devoted much of the past decade to analysing the relative effects of red in sport, their premise being that the incidence of successful players or teams that play in red was simply too high to be attributed to pure chance. Initially, they looked at the outcomes of four combat sports at the 2004 Olympic Games in Athens – Taekwondo, Boxing, Greco-Roman Wrestling and Freestyle Wrestling, events where the participants are randomly given red or blue clothing or body protection to fight in. In bouts where there was a large points difference and clearly one better fighter, the colour of the clothing was irrelevant, but in those contests where both fighters appeared to be equally matched, the number of wins for the contestant in red was significantly higher.[3]

Later, in an article published in the *Journal of Sports Sciences* in 2008, Hill and Barton expanded their study to include the teams in the old First Division and Premier League football between 1947 and 2003. In keeping with previous results, they once more discovered that those teams wearing a predominantly red first-choice kit had a disproportionately higher rate of success in their home games (while wearing the red strip), and were more likely to end each season as the winner of the championship. Indeed, of the 65 winners of the top flight in England during the post-war era, some 41 have won red kits. "Across a range of sports," they announced, "we find that wearing red is consistently associated with a higher probability of winning."[4]

In football especially, the incidence of successful teams wearing red is extremely persuasive: Bayern Munich of Germany, Italy's AC Milan, Benfica in Portugal and, internationally, the World and European champions, Spain. Indeed, given the weight of evidence in the case for red kits or uniforms, it's surprising that more teams do not simply switch colours to help increase their chances. In June 2012, Cardiff City Football Club announced they were changing their home kit from blue – a colour they had worn since 1910 – to red as part of a deal with the club's new Malaysian investors. Red is the national colour of Malaysia and is also seen as a lucky colour. Although the change met with widespread hostility from fans – after all, they are nicknamed 'the Bluebirds' – the move, though primarily financial, also reaped some strangely significant results. At the time of writing, for instance, Cardiff City have played ten home games in the Football League Championship wearing the new red kit and, intriguingly, they have won every match, scoring 21 goals and conceding just five. It is moreover the best home record in all of European fooball, and has helped Cardiff to the top of table.

For every red success story, though, there's a counter-argument to suggest that maybe wearing red isn't the be-all and end-all when it comes to achieving sporting success. Take the Great Britain and Northern Ireland team in the London 2012 Olympics, for example. Their team outfit for the Games was created by the renowned fashion designer Stella McCartney, but immediately drew criticism not simply because of the predominance of blue and white (rather than red) and the fact that it seemed to go against all commonly-held beliefs concerning the impact of colour in sport, but also because it was perceived as being unpatriotic. But the result was that Team GB exceeded all expectations: they won a record total of 65 medals, took third in the final medal table and registered their greatest performance at the modern-day Games in over 100 years.

Yet it's not just the colours that players or teams dress in that can help determine the level of performance they achieve. Other research suggests that wearing certain colours not only determines how successful you are, but also the manner in which you compete. In 1988, Mark G. Frank and Thomas Gilovich of Cornell University published their paper, 'The Dark Side of Self and Social Perception: Black Uniform and Aggression in Professional Sports', their contention being that black was forever regarded as the colour associated with the suspect, the inappropriate and ultimately, the evil. Reputations, they argued, are "blackened". Dubious club members are "blackballed" or "blacklisted". Even the bad guys in American Westerns always wear a black hat. And when the Chicago White Sox threw the 1919 World Series as part of a betting scam, they were soon re-cast as the "Chicago *Black* Sox".

Frank and Gilovich believed that the connotations that came hand-in-hand with the colour black could also materially affect the nature of a sportsperson's performance. Initially, the pair examined the disciplinary and penalty records of the National Football League (NFL) and the National Hockey League (NHL) from 1970 through to 1986 (the last completed season before they published their paper), to establish whether there was any correlation between the colour of a team's kit or uniform and how well behaved they were on the field of play. They awarded teams points for each transgression or penalty given against them during play and created a 'league table' of offenders.

What they found was remarkable. In the NFL, for example, the five teams with the highest 'Malevolence Rating' all played in black uniforms, while in the NHL five of the top six in the table also wore black kits. The question, of course, was whether the more aggressive players were, in some way, attracted to playing for teams that played in black or if referees, or umpires were more likely to penalise those in black because of some subconscious association of the colour with all things unfair and even evil. Frank tested the theory still further in taking two groups of volunteers, one dressed in white and the other in black. The groups were then shown a description of various games and pastimes and asked to indicate which ones appealed to them. Intriguingly, those dressed in black tended to go for the more confrontational games ('dart gun duel', for example), whereas those in white preferred less combative games such as 'putting contests'.[5]

With this in mind then, it would seem that the ideal colours for a successful player or team would be red and black – presumably because the combination of a supposedly dominant colour like red, married to an aggressive colour such as black, could only serve to intimidate opponents and referees alike; an idea that may explain why Manchester United are the most successful team in English football, but singularly fails to explain why a team like Brentford, who play in a predominantly red strip with elements of black, have never come close to landing English football's greatest prize.

NOTES & SOURCES

1. *www.bbc.co.uk/news/health-10767128.*
2. *'Signal Content of Red Facial Coloration in Female Mandrills (Mandrillus sphinx)',* 2006, *Joanna M. Setchell, Jean E. Wickings and Leslie A. Knapp.*
3. *'Red Enhances Human Performance in Contests',* 2005, *Russell A. Hill and Robert A. Barton*
4. *'Red shirt colour is associated with long-term team success in English football',* 2008, *Martin J. Attrill, Karen A. Gresty, Russell A. Hill and Robert A. Barton.*
5. Journal of Personality and Social Psychology, *1988, Vol. 54, 'The Dark Side of Self and Social Perception: Black Uniform and Aggression in Professional Sports', Mark G. Frank and Thomas Gilovich.*

10. CAUGHT SPEEDING
Just how fast can humans hope to run the 100m?

At the inaugural modern-day Olympic Games in Athens of 1896, Thomas Burke of the United States won the 100 metres gold medal in a time of 12 seconds dead. Burke stood out from the rest of the field in the sprint races because of his unorthodox crouching start, a tactic which gave him a distinct advantage in getting away quickly at the gun.

Today, the crouching start in the sprints is used by every sprinter, but Burke's determination to seek out whatever competitive advantage he could find certainly paid dividends, not least because he went on to win his preferred event, the 400m, as well. In the intervening 116 years since his victory, sprinters have continued to try and discover ways and means to become even faster. Some have been inspired, others not so. Some methods have been legal, while others, famously, have proved quite the opposite.

But in such a powerful and explosive sport, where the tiniest fraction of a second makes all the difference between winning and losing, the quest to become the fastest on the planet continues to fascinate sports fans the world over, and while the 100m has always been the must-see event of any Olympic Games or World Championships, it has been Usain Bolt's performances in recent years that have elevated the race to new and unheralded heights.

Yes, occasionally in sport there are those rare moments that leave you awe-struck, mouth agape, and the 100m at the Beijing Olympics of 2008 was certainly one of those. Aged just 21, Jamaica's Bolt not only become the first man in history to go under 9.7 seconds but also accomplished this feat in such an unimaginably effortless manner that it left commentators and experts alike wondering what they had just witnessed. Though the watching world was understandably astounded by what Bolt had just done, many felt frustration as the 6'5" (1.95 metres) Jamaican had slowed down markedly in the final 15 metres and began celebrating his victory. Soon after the Olympics, however, a team of scientists at the University of Oslo, Norway, analysed TV footage of the race they had collated from a range of international broadcasters and attempted to calculate the time Bolt would have run had he kept going at his maximum speed until the very end of the race. Eventually, they concluded that he would have crossed the line in 9.55 seconds.[1]

This was an unfathomable time and one which, had he achieved it, would have knocked nearly two-tenths of a second off Bolt's own world record of 9.72 seconds – an eternity in sprinting. As it was, Bolt returned to action the following year, and at the IAAF World Championships in Berlin – only this time he kept on running, taking the gold medal in 9.58 seconds. It was not only .11s better than his own astonishing world record – the largest-ever margin cut from the world record since digital timing began in 1977 – but he was also .13s ahead of the USA's Tyson Gay in second place.

Bolt's time in Beijing should not have arrived until 2030, while his 9.58 seconds in Berlin wouldn't have happened until 2100.

What made Bolt's times so extraordinary was that if the world record had progressed at the rate it already had throughout the remainder of the twentieth century, then his time in Beijing should not have arrived until 2030, while his 9.58 seconds in Berlin wouldn't have happened until 2100. The manner in which he ran the races was key. In his book *The Perfection Point*, John Brenkus studied Bolt's win in Beijing and found that if you split that 100m into ten x 10m sections, Bolt ran four of those sections faster than any athlete in history had ever completed a single 10m chunk.[2]

Certainly it was a remarkable race – and pace – but Bolt's systematic evisceration of the record books was such that times previously thought unobtainable by the experts were apparently now within reach. His success had not only made people think about how fast Usain Bolt could go, but how fast man might go in the future. Bolt himself has said that he could one day envisage running a time of 9.4 seconds in the 100m and certainly, if he were to put together the perfect race, there is every chance he could do so. After all, his start is still noticeably slower than that of his rivals, thereby costing him hundredths of a second, and his tendency to coast over the finishing line once assured of victory has often cost him hundredths and, occasionally, tenths of a second. Moreover, at the 100m final in Beijing, he even ran the race with his shoelace undone!

But there is scientific evidence to suggest that 9.4 seconds may be outside human capability. In 2008, Dr Mark Denny of Stanford University in the US published a paper analysing the highest speeds achieved in running events, from sprinting right through to the marathon, with some going back as far as 1900. Using a statistical technique called 'extreme-value analysis', Denny examined the trends in how times had improved over the last century, and discerned that in the 100m the maximum human speed limit is 10.55 metres per second (allowing for a slower start), a speed that when applied to the 100m would give a maximum time of 9.48 seconds.[3]

As with most scientific studies, there are those who beg to differ, though. John Barrow, a professor of mathematical sciences at Cambridge University, believes there is an additional four hundredths of a second to be found, especially in the case of Bolt. In an article in *Significance*, the magazine of the Royal Statistical Society and the American Statistical Association, Barrow argues if a sprinter as talented as Bolt could improve his start to the point where he could respond as quickly as possible without triggering a false start, then he could take an additional 0.05 seconds off his time.[4] Secondly, if he were to benefit from a stronger tailwind of up to the legal limit of 2m/s – his run in Berlin had just a 0.9m/s supporting breeze – he could theoretically benefit from less drag and therefore reduce his time by another 0.06 seconds. Finally, by running at a higher altitude with a lower air density, another 0.03 seconds might be saved. When the Olympic Games were held in Mexico City in 1968 at 2,240m (7,349 feet) above sea level, there were some marked improvements in events over shorter distances, and while definitive world records are only permitted up to heights of 1,000m, this still gives an even greater chance for a quicker time.

Of course while experts and scientists alike debate just how fast Bolt can go, the truth is that he himself may only have one more Olympic Games left in him – Rio de Janeiro in 2016 – by which time he will be nearly 30 and in all likelihood past his prime.

Usain Bolt has already succeeded in reshaping the wider debate about the physical limitations of human beings.

Whether he goes faster or not remains to be seen but even if he doesn't, then memorable world records aside, he has already succeeded in reshaping the wider debate about the physical limitations of human beings.

Over time, there may well be developments and progress in peripheral issues such as the running shoes of the sprinters or the technology employed in manufacturing the track, but here a theory exists to suggest that human beings could run significantly faster. A study by the University of Wyoming's Dr Matthew Bundle in the *Journal of Applied Physiology* showed how a human's speed is governed more by contracting muscle fibres than by the sheer force of running. It is the muscle fibres that are responsible for getting your feet off the ground and if humans learn to do this more efficiently, argues Bundle, it could signal huge increases in their potential speed.

Bundle and his team tested their theory using a high-speed treadmill capable of reaching speeds of over 40mph which could also measure the forces applied to the surface as each runner's foot made contact with it. They then had their subjects perform at high speeds but using different running styles, and discovered that the ground forces applied while hopping on one leg, for example, exceeded those applied during more normal top speed running by 30 per cent or more; while the forces generated by the muscles within the leg were roughly 1.5 to two times greater as well. This, argued Bundle, proved that the limit of an individual's running speed is set by the muscle fibres, in that the speed of those fibres determine just how quickly the sprinter's leg can apply force to the track. Using these findings, Bundle estimated that theoretically, a human could run as fast as 40mph, or over 12mph faster than Bolt at his top speed. Indeed, were he capable of such speeds, he would then run the 100m in just 6.7 seconds, crossing the line just as Bolt reached the 60-metre mark.[5] Maybe then, and

HOW USAIN BOLT COMPARES TO THE ANIMAL KINGDOM OVER 100M...

Even the fastest man on the planet trails behind the animal kingdom's speed kings.

100m

USAIN BOLT
9.58SECS

OSTRICH
6.7SECS

CHEETAH
5.8SECS

11 SECS   10   9   8   7   6   5

Source: LiveScience.com

PAST AND (POSSIBLE) FUTURE OLYMPIC MEN'S 100M TIMES

There has been incredible improvement over 100 years but scientists predict we can go much faster...

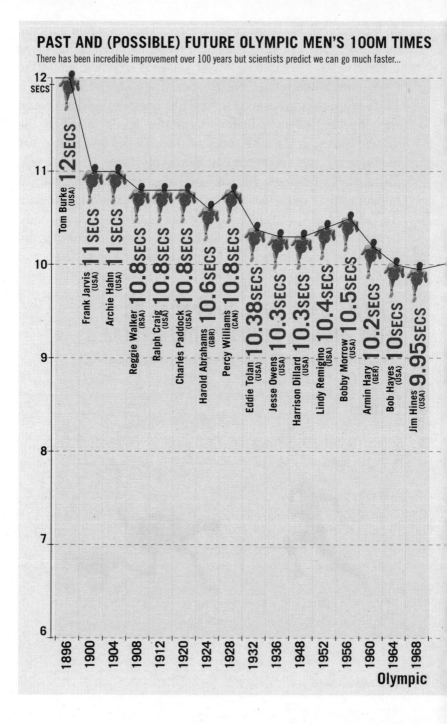

Tom Burke (USA) 12 SECS

Frank Jarvis (USA) 11 SECS

Archie Hahn (USA) 11 SECS

Reggie Walker (RSA) 10.8 SECS

Ralph Craig (USA) 10.8 SECS

Charles Paddock (USA) 10.8 SECS

Harold Abrahams (GBR) 10.6 SECS

Percy Williams (CAN) 10.8 SECS

Eddie Tolan (USA) 10.38 SECS

Jesse Owens (USA) 10.3 SECS

Harrison Dillard (USA) 10.3 SECS

Lindy Remigino (USA) 10.4 SECS

Bobby Morrow (USA) 10.5 SECS

Armin Hary (GER) 10.2 SECS

Bob Hayes (USA) 10 SECS

Jim Hines (USA) 9.95 SECS

Y-axis: 12 SECS, 11, 10, 9, 8, 7, 6

X-axis: 1896, 1900, 1904, 1908, 1912, 1920, 1924, 1928, 1932, 1936, 1948, 1952, 1956, 1960, 1964, 1968 — **Olympic**

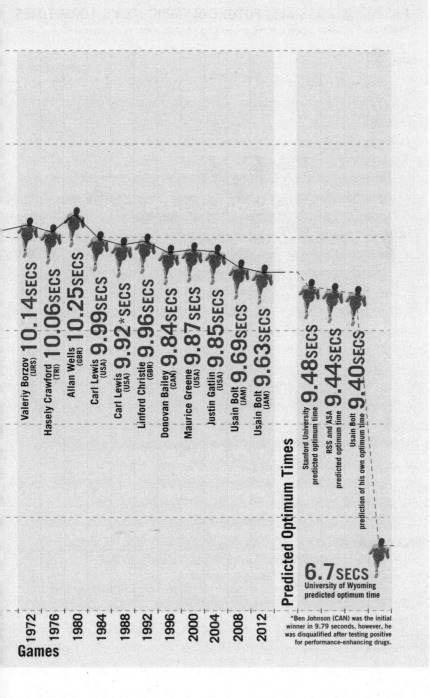

Valeriy Borzov (URS) 10.14 SECS
Hasely Crawford (TRI) 10.06 SECS
Allan Wells (GBR) 10.25 SECS
Carl Lewis (USA) 9.99 SECS
Carl Lewis (USA) 9.92* SECS
Linford Christie (GBR) 9.96 SECS
Donovan Bailey (CAN) 9.84 SECS
Maurice Greene (USA) 9.87 SECS
Justin Gatlin (USA) 9.85 SECS
Usain Bolt (JAM) 9.69 SECS
Usain Bolt (JAM) 9.63 SECS

Predicted Optimum Times

Stanford University predicted optimum time 9.48 SECS
RSS and ASA predicted optimum time 9.44 SECS
Usain Bolt prediction of his own optimum time 9.40 SECS

6.7 SECS
University of Wyoming
predicted optimum time

1972
1976
1980
1984
1988
1992
1996
2000
2004
2008
2012

Games

*Ben Johnson (CAN) was the initial
winner in 9.79 seconds, however, he
was disqualified after testing positive
for performance-enhancing drugs.

only then, would Usain Bolt know how it feels for everyone else who has to compete against him.

NOTES & SOURCES

1. 'How Fast could Usain Bolt Have Run? A Dynamical Study', 2008, H. K. Eriksen, J. R. Kristiansen, Ø. Langangen, I. K. Wehus

2. The Perfection Point: Sport Science Predicts the Fastest Man, the Highest Jump, and the Limits of Athletic Performance, 2010, John Brenkus.

3. www.economist.com/node/21559903.

4. Significance, the magazine of the Royal Statistical Society and the American Statistical Association; Journal of Applied Physiology.

5. Journal of Applied Physiology, Dr Martin Bundle, University of Wyoming, 2010.

11. BAGS FOR LIFE
Is Steve Williams really New Zealand's highest-earning sports star?

No one sets out to become a caddy, not really. Frustrated players who have fallen short of a career in the professional game, supportive siblings or just mates at a loose end… they can all end up carrying the bag for a golfer and more often than not, carrying the can when it all goes horribly wrong.

Manual labourer and club cleaner on one hand, confidant and counsellor on the other, it's the caddy's job to be there by his employer's side through good times and bad. This unique band of brothers (and occasionally sisters) travels the world together, celebrating and commiserating in equal measure, but it can be a hard life and the trick to being a successful caddy is not how well you do your job (although obviously important), but *who* you end up carrying a bag for. Typically, caddies are paid a basic salary and then receive a cut of the player's prize money. In the US this is $1,000 (£624) a week as the base salary and then 5 per cent of any winnings. If a player finishes in the top-10 places, however, this cut rises to 7 per cent and if the player wins the tournament outright the caddie can expect 10 per cent of the golfer's prize money.[1]

Theoretically, that sounds like a good deal for the bagmen and women, but remember, caddies are also responsible for their own expenses, including travel and accommodation, which can amount to around 25 per cent of their annual income. For those on a bag of one of the top players, this doesn't present a problem as they can expect to earn hundreds of thousands of dollars for a season's work, but it might prove a tough existence indeed for anyone assisting at the wrong end of the money lists. Not that

Steve Williams had any such concerns while working with Tiger Woods. The Kiwi caddied for the record-breaking American from 1999 to 2011 and was by his side for 13 of his 14 major victories. In that time Woods won 64 times on the PGA Tour alone, taking nearly £56 million ($90 million) in prize money; so while he was sitting pretty, so too was Williams, who earned an estimated £7.5 million ($12 million) before the pair split in somewhat acrimonious circumstances in July 2011.[2]

For years it was widely believed that Steve Williams was New Zealand's highest-earning sportsman, even though all he did was carry a bag for Woods. In 2006, for example, he earned an estimated £792,000 ($1.27 million). Had he been a player, this would have put him comfortably in the world's top 75, ahead of the likes of Freddie Couples, Justin Leonard and Bubba Watson.[3] But was Williams really the biggest earner in New Zealand sport? Well, disregarding the argument that he was not a playing participant, we can see that there were several stars comfortably ahead of Williams at the height of his (or rather Woods') success, most notably in the shape of sailing's Russell Coutts and Brad Butterworth, whose exploits in the America's Cup have taken them to the very pinnacle of their sport.

It was widely believed that Steve Williams was New Zealand's highest-earning sportsman, even though all he did was carry a bag for Woods.

The country's cricketers, meanwhile, have also benefited from the recent emergence of the lucrative Indian Premier League, a competition paying salaries far in excess of anything else in the game. For a player such as Kiwi all-rounder Daniel Vettori, who already earned around NZ$300,000 (£153,000/US$246,000) a year as national team skipper, this can mean a huge boost. In 2011, for example, he signed a lucrative £343,000 (US$552,000) deal with the Royal Challengers Bangalore.

Interestingly, the national sport of New Zealand – Rugby Union – fails to register, and the sport's two highest-earning players –

QUIDS-IN KIWIS

Or why Steve Williams wasn't the biggest earner in New Zealand sport.

RUSSELL COUTTS (Sailing)
$12.2 million (£7.6 million)

BRAD BUTTERWORTH (Sailing)
$6.5 million (£4 million)

RYAN NELSEN (Football)
$7.2 million (£4.5 million)

SCOTT DIXON (Indy Racing)
$4.8 million (£3 million)

MICHAEL CAMPBELL (Golf)
$3.2 million (£2 million)

STEVE WILLIAMS (Caddy)
$1.27 million (£792,000)

CHRIS KILLEN (Football)
$1.2 million (£748,000)

SEAN MARKS (Basketball)
$1.2 million (£748,000)

DANIEL VETTORI (Cricket)
$850,000 (£530,000)

Note: Figures in US dollars based on 2007/08 earnings.

fly-half Dan Carter and flanker and national team captain Richie McCaw – have only as recently as 2010 received guaranteed retainers from New Zealand Rugby Union of NZ$750,000 a year (£385,000/US$620,000). While undeniably a healthy salary, it's not a patch on carrying a golf bag for a living.

NOTES & SOURCES

1. *Dennis Cone, Professional Caddies' Association.*
2. *www.pgatour.com.*
3. *www.forbes.com, June 6, 2007.*

12. CAN SPORTING INEPTITUDE MAKE MONEY?
Turning epic sporting failure into financial gain

For all the indisputable examples of excellence in the annals of sport, there are just as many cases where the lack of quality, or indeed absence of any apparent talent whatsoever, prove that it's not merely the gifted who grab the gold. Yes, there is serious money to be made from incompetence in sport, irrespective of whether it's a seasoned performer suddenly undone by a momentary and humiliating lapse of concentration, or an ill-equipped rookie thrown into the lions' den to create a spectacle in front of the watching world.

For the most part, sports fans always embrace the epic loser. Maybe it's the golfer who chokes, such as Northern Ireland's Rory McIlroy, blowing a four-shot lead on the final day of a major.[1] Or the gifted snooker player, like Jimmy White, who reaches six World Championship finals but loses every one.[2] Or the footballer, like Gareth Southgate, who misses the key penalty in a crucial shoot-out, depriving his success-starved country of the glory they've coveted for so long.[3]

It's the vulnerability that makes them so lovable and, indeed, so very marketable. Take Andy Murray. Often criticised for being dour and grumpy, the young Scot became the first Brit in 74 years to make the final of the Wimbledon Men's Singles Championship in 2012 and though he fell in four sets to Switzerland's Roger Federer, it was his emotional speech after the match, full of tears and no small amount of good humour, that suddenly endeared him to a new legion of fans. According to the marketing expert Ian Monks, Murray was now a "loser perceived by the world as a winner" and a player who had "served an ace for his marketing and PR teams."[4]

For someone like Murray, who has had the misfortune to be playing professional tennis at the same time as three of the greatest players in history, it wasn't a calculated move to somehow reinvent his public persona but merely the inevitable outpourings of a player who had come so close, only to fail once more. Besides, he didn't need the sympathy, nor did he need the money.[5]

Of course, Murray's marketability improved still further when, just one month after that Wimbledon defeat, he managed to turn the trauma of his fourth Grand Slam final defeat into glorious victory as he took the gold medal at the London 2012 Olympic Games, vanquishing Federer in straight sets on Centre Court. Then five weeks later, he went one better: winning the US Open to become the first British man since 1936 to secure a Grand Slam singles event. Now, with

According to the marketing expert Ian Monks, [Andy] Murray was now a "loser perceived by the world as a winner" and a player who had "served an ace for his marketing and PR teams."

a medal round his neck, a hoodoo laid to rest and a smile on his face, Murray has ticked all the marketing boxes. Which is precisely what differentiates him from those sporting losers who face defeat not merely because they're pitted against players who are better than them, but because they lack the talent to even mount anything like a challenge in the first place. Some, like Trevor Misipeka, the 22-stone (140 kilograms) American-Samoan shot putter who found himself running in the 100m sprint at the World Athletics Championships in Edmonton of 2001 (he finished in 14.28 seconds – almost 4s behind the winner, Kim Collins) enjoy only a brief spell in the limelight. Others, such as the Olympic swimmer from Equatorial Guinea, Eric 'the Eel' Moussambani, also find global fame but fail to financially capitalise on their new-found celebrity.[6]

But it takes a special (or very ordinary) someone to turn sporting ignominy into a life-changing new income stream, and perhaps the most apposite example is that of the ski jumper Eddie 'the Eagle' Edwards, a plasterer from Cheltenham, Gloucestershire. In 1988, Edwards had arrived at the Winter Olympic Games in Calgary, Canada, having just taken out a £1,000 ($1,600) bank loan to fund his trip. Without any sponsorship – he had taken additional part-time jobs waiting tables and cleaning floors to help pay his way – Edwards nevertheless managed to take his place in the starting line-up for the ski jump, but the step-up in standard soon found him wanting. Even though he was the UK's number-one ranked ski jumper, he still came dead last in both the 70m and the 90m.

While success on the ramp had eluded Edwards – the press now called him a "ski dropper" – his efforts had attracted worldwide recognition and even while he was at the Games the offers were already rolling in.

But while success on the ramp had eluded Edwards – the press now called him a "ski dropper" – his efforts had attracted worldwide recognition and even while he was at the Games, the offers were already rolling in. Indeed, by the time he left, he had around £85,000 ($136,000) of commercial contracts already signed – and all without the need for a manager or agent scrutinising the small print.

On his return to the UK, Edwards was feted as though he had actually won a gold and the opportunities to cash in on his newfound fame continued to pour in. There were television commercials and personal appearances at nightclubs; he opened new rides at theme parks; and the *Daily Mail* newspaper even paid him £45,000 ($72,000) for the rights to his life story. In one day, admittedly one *long* day, Edwards maintains he earned £65,000 ($104,000) from a string of personal appearances and commercial commitments. Suddenly Eddie Edwards, a plasterer from Gloucestershire, had gone from earning £6,000 ($9,660) a year to a reported £10,000 ($16,000) an hour and in the 12 months that followed his dismal showing in the Winter Olympics, he had earned himself an estimated £600,000 ($966,000). But the success didn't last: by 1989, Edwards annual income fell to around £150,000 ($240,000), and then again in 1990, down to £90,000 ($145,000). By 1992, he was faced with a mammoth tax bill that he simply couldn't pay and he was subsequently declared bankrupt.[7]

What this example shows is not just how profitable mediocrity can be but how, when coupled with charisma and/or pity, it can lead to almost instant reward. Yet it wasn't really Edwards' lack of prowess on the ramp that endeared him to the world, it was his indefatigability. For all his cartoon capers in the snow, he was, after all, the British record holder at the ski jump, even if that meant he was some way behind the more established jumpers and nations to compete at the 1988 Winter Games. No, what his 'talent' gave him was a window of opportunity, a spell in the limelight that he quite rightly took full advantage of.

Arguably the greatest ski jumper in history... Matti Nykänen ended up doing all the same things as the man who came 57 places below him in Calgary.

Contrast Edwards' continuing popularity[8] with the man who won both the 70m and 90m ramp at Calgary in 1988, Finland's Matti Nykänen. Arguably, the greatest ski jumper in history – he won four Olympic gold medals, five World Championship titles, four World Cup tour championships and 46 individual World Cup circuit victories – Nykänen's marketability waned after his jumping career ended, not least because he went spectacularly off the rails. Beset by marital and financial problems (largely because of his three divorce settlements), Nykänen, like Edwards, found himself promoting products, making personal appearances and releasing his own records.[9] For a spell he worked as a stripper and advised callers on a premium rate sex chat-line.[10] Like Edwards, he too struggled to pay his tax bills and in 2006, a biopic of his life – *Matti* – was released.[11] In short, he ended up doing all the same things as the man who came 57 places below him in Calgary.

Unlike Edwards, though, Nykänen also spent time in prison as he was jailed for 26 months following a stabbing incident in 2004, and then another 16 months after aggravated assault on his fourth wife, Mervi, in 2009 – events that naturally dented his earnings potential.

NOTES & SOURCES

1. *Rory McIlroy began the final round of the 2011 Masters at Augusta with a four-shot lead but dropped six shots in three holes on the back nine on his way to an eight-over-par 80 as South Africa's Charl Schwartzel won the Green Jacket. In the next major, the US Open at Congressional, McIlroy romped to an eight-shot victory.*

2. *Jimmy White reached six finals of the World Snooker Championship (including five consecutively, from 1990–94) but lost them all despite being acknowledged as the most gifted player of his generation.*

3. *Having missed the key penalty in the Euro 96 semi-final against Germany, Gareth Southgate appeared in a Pizza Hut advertisement of 1996 alongside Stuart Pearce and Chris Waddle, two former England players who had also missed spot-kicks for the national team in the World Cup semi-final of 1990.*

4. *www.Brand Republic, July 12, 2012.*

5. *As of July 23, 2012, Andy Murray's career prize money stood at £13,388,639 ($21,555,708) (www.atpworldtour.com).*

6. *Eric Moussambani completed his 100m freestyle heat at the 2000 Olympic Games in Sydney in 1:52.72. His time was more than double that of the other competitors in the race and was also outside the world record for the 200m event.*

7. *Eddie the Eagle: 'I Went From £6,000 a Year to £10,000 an Hour', Daily Telegraph, February 19, 2012.*

8. *At the time of writing, plans are afoot to make a biopic of Edwards' life, with Steve Coogan said to be taking the lead role (news.bbc.co.uk/1/hi/ entertainment/6937217.stm).*

9. *Plans were once mooted for Matti Nykänen and Eddie Edwards to record an album together. Everyone wants a piece of Matti, Tommi Nieminen and Riku Siivonen, Helsingin Sanomat, August 8, 2004.*

10. *www.guardian.co.uk/global/2010/jan/07/matti-nykanen-ski-finland-olympics.*

11. Matti: Hell Is for Heroes, *directed by Aleksi Mäkelä and written by Marko Leino, Solar Films, 2006.*

13. ANIMAL ATHLETES
The costs and rewards of owning a greyhound, racehorse or racing pigeon

While it's the dream of many to own their own racehorse, the costs involved are often prohibitive. With the median cost of a racehorse in the UK being £15,000 ($24,000) and the cost of keeping it in training around £16,000 ($26,000) per annum[1], it can be a frightening prospect for those whose pockets are not that cavernous. It's easier – and significantly cheaper – to dip your toe in the water of competitive animal racing by buying a greyhound instead, not least because there are no jockey fees to consider.

Your first step is to actually buy the dog and the price of a greyhound varies depending on its age, breeding and ability. A puppy yet to race will sell for between £350 ($564) and £1,500 ($2,415), although no dog is allowed to race until it is at least 15 months old. Older dogs with a proven track record can sell for up to £5,000 ($8,000), and occasionally those who have already won high-class, or 'Category 1' races can fetch upward of £20,000 ($32,000)[2].It must also be remembered that the racing career of a greyhound is very short, with most dogs retiring between the ages of three and five.

Once you've bought your dog, you'll have to register it with the Greyhound Board of Great Britain if you intend to race it. This costs £26 ($42), although if it's already registered and you want to change its racing name, this will cost an additional £81 ($130). You'll then have to find a trainer. On average, training a greyhound with a reputable trainer costs around £6 ($10) per day, plus any additional fees incurred for veterinary and medical bills.

When your dog begins racing, you and your trainer will also be subject to a raft of regulations laid down by the Department for Environment, Food and Rural Affairs (DEFRA) and you will need to purchase a transport cage that conforms to these guidelines, with the size depending on whether the journey being taken is under or over eight hours. Think of it as your horsebox – only one that won't reduce the economy of your car and shouldn't cost you more than £100 ($160)! Unlike a domestic dog, feeding the animal isn't so easy either. With the highest power-to-weight ratio of any canine, greyhounds need a diet of low bulk and high energy, with carefully limited amounts of crude proteins and fats so as to maintain the body weight and therefore their speed. With most greyhounds racing once every five to seven days, an owner needs its dog to win just one race a month to cover all running costs.[3]

The most prestigious of all races is the annual Greyhound Derby held at Wimbledon. Win that race with your dog and you could even buy yourself a racehorse.

There are a total of around 70,000 races each year at the UK's 26 major greyhound tracks.[4] Of these, there are four to five Category 1 races, held over one to four rounds of races, which carry a minimum prize of £12,500 ($20,215) for the eventual winners, with the first-placed dog in one of the heats assured a minimum of £100 ($160). Category 2 races, meanwhile, are contested over one to three rounds and offer a minimum first prize of £5,000 ($8,000), with heat winners also receiving at least £100. Finally, Category 3 events – the lowest-ranked races – are over one or two rounds and offer a minimum first prize of £1,000 ($1,600).[5]

The most prestigious of all races, however, is the annual Greyhound Derby held at Wimbledon. In 2012, Blonde Snapper took the title and the £125,000 ($201,250) in prize money. Win that race with your dog and you could even buy yourself a racehorse.

But there may be an even better way to invest that money. If you already have a horse – *any* female horse – you could take a punt and let her breed with a proven winner in the hope that she produces offspring that go on to become champions in their own right. Take Frankel, the undefeated stallion who won all 14 of his races (including an unprecedented world record-equalling nine consecutive Grade 1 race wins) and retired in October 2012. Considered by some experts the greatest racehorse of all time, Frankel's worth now derives not from his ability to win races and prize money but his ability to sire offspring, and in his first year at stud at Banstead Manor in Suffolk, England, he is expected to 'cover' some 100 mares. The initial fee charged for letting him attend to your mare is £125,000 ($201,250).[6] It will take at least three years to find out, but if Frankel's first crop of colts and fillies are successful, the figure will rise.

Even successful greyhounds also provide an opportunity to make their owners money long after their last race has been run. Stud fees for greyhounds range from £400–£1,200 (£644–£1,932)[7] and with a greyhound able to perform at least twice a week, your four-legged companion can provide an earnings potential in excess of £120,000 ($193,200).

Racing pigeons also have investment potential. You can buy a good quality racing pigeon from a reputable breeder for as little £20 ($32) and a bird can live up to 20 years if it is well looked after. A street pigeon, by comparison, will only live between three and four years[7]. But there is some significant money to be made if you have a successful pigeon. While smaller club races over shorter distances will generally only offer trophies and kudos as prizes, the end-of-season 'one loft' race typically offers a first prize of £20,000 ($32,000). The most lucrative race of all, though, is the annual Million Dollar Pigeon Race in South Africa, an event which, as the name suggests, boasts a prize fund that is more in keeping with a golf tournament or a title fight in boxing.[9]

More recently, there has been a surge in demand for racing pigeons in China where the sport is positively booming. Today, there are 300,000 members of the Chinese Racing Pigeon Association and the market for birds there is such that birds that used to cost £400 ($644) five years ago now cost in excess of £2,500

($4,025) and sometimes much, much more. In January 2012, for example, the Belgian racing pigeon dealer Pigeon Paradise sold one bird to a Chinese buyer for £207,000 ($333,270).[10]

  The only issue is whether your prized pigeon actually finds its way home. In August 2012, a race from Galashiels in Scotland to Thirsk in North Yorkshire saw just 13 of the 232 birds make it back to their owners[11] which is easier to stomach if your pigeon only cost £20 ($32) but less so if you splashed out nearly a quarter of a million.

NOTES & SOURCES

1. *www.britishhorseracing.com.*
2. *www.thedogs.co.uk/BuyingGreyhounds.aspx*
3. *'Feeding the Racing Greyhound for Performance', John Kohnke BVSc, RDA*
4. *www.thedogs.co.uk*
5. *www.gbgb.org.uk.*
6. *www.bbc.co.uk/sport/0/horse-racing/20326577.*
7. *www.greyhound-data.com.*
8. *www.rpra.org*
9. *www.scmdpr.com*
10. The Economist, *27/10/12*
11. *www.bbc.co.uk/news/uk-scotland-south-scotland-19343027*

14. WHAT IF FIFA WAS A COUNTRY?

It's a huge organisation but what would happen if FIFA became its own state?

Though sport, in all its magnificent guises, continues to preoccupy people the world over, it's worth remembering that it is not something that just happens or some entirely natural, pre-ordained event; there is no sporting alchemy that suddenly occurs when two players or teams get together. Yes, behind every great sport is a governing body tasked with taking care of the really dull stuff, from officiating and funding to legislation and planning.

It's not easy being an administrator in sport. Get it right and you won't hear a word of praise; get things wrong and you won't hear the end of it. For many sports fans, the organisations that run their favourite games are often perceived as little more than office blocks of grey-suited, bureaucratic busybodies, detached from the game with little or no interest or appreciation of the concerns of the ordinary supporter. Like them or loathe them, the world of sport would be nothing without these officials and in the case of the biggest sports, such as football, it takes a suitably large organisation to give every player, team and club a common purpose and to make the game one of the few sports that can now genuinely lay claim to being a global one.

From its headquarters in Zurich, Switzerland, the Fédération Internationale de Football Association (FIFA) oversees the global game of football. The reach of this not-for-profit charity is staggering. It boasts some 209 affiliated national associations thereby making it, theoretically, a bigger organisation than the United Nations, which has just 193 member states. Indeed, there are just eight sovereign nations in the world that are not part of the FIFA family.[1]

With so many national associations affiliated to FIFA, it's hardly surprising that the body can lay claim to having some 265 million players (male and female) in addition to 5 million referees and officials in its global constituency. It's a 'population' that represents around 4 per cent of the planet's total population, theoretically making FIFA the fourth most populous 'nation' in the world, just behind the US and marginally ahead of Indonesia.[2] Curiously, the size of the FIFA workforce shows a 'civil service' that amounts to just 310 people globally, compared to nearly half a million that help run the UK.[3]

It's a position that gives FIFA some genuine power and not merely in the sport it oversees. If, for instance, you want your country to stage their blue-riband event, the FIFA World Cup Finals, then you must modify your nation's fiscal laws to make FIFA exempt from any taxes ordinarily due, but also make the players themselves exempt from taxes that would be levied on their sponsorships and endorsements, should they play in the event. "Any host country requires a comprehensive tax exemption to be given to FIFA and further parties involved in the hosting and staging of an event," said a FIFA spokesman in May, 2010.[4] Moreover, as a body with charitable status, FIFA also pays little or no tax locally on its revenues either.

It's a 'population' that represents around 4 per cent of the planet's total population, theoretically making FIFA the fourth most populous 'nation' in the world.

Behind FIFA's virtually tax-free existence and the concomitant array of extremely favourable financial perks from which it benefits, lies an organisation that is not so much the keeper of 'the Beautiful Game' as a money-making machine *par excellence*. When FIFA publishes its full financial results, it does so based on a four-year cycle, the final year coinciding with that of a World Cup Finals tournament. In the last cycle, from

2007–10, their total event-related revenue was £2.611 billion ($4.203 billion) and total expenditure was £2.218 billion ($3.557 billion), giving football's governing a body a 'profit' of £393 million ($632 million).[5] If that figure seems comparatively small beer, given that it represents four years of 'trading', it should be borne in mind that when FIFA published their latest annual report, in 2011, it also showed they were holding cash reserves of some £798 million ($1.28 billion).[6] Given this was a negative figure less than a decade ago – they were, in effect, overdrawn – it's some savings plan. From those reserves alone, FIFA received £31.8 million ($51 million) in interest.[7]

But where does the money come from? Not from donations or grants (like most charities) or annual subscriptions, or 'taxes' from its affiliated associations. No, it comes almost entirely from the FIFA World Cup Finals, a quadrennial tournament that is behind only the Summer Olympic Games for the honour of being the world's biggest sporting event. But while the two events stand comparison in their global appeal – an estimated 715 million watched the 2010 World Cup Final on television, while a little over 619 million saw the Opening Ceremony of the 2012 Olympic Games in London, England[8] – the disparity in the ability of the hosts (or rather FIFA) to make money from the event couldn't be much greater. In recent times, only the 1984 Games in Los Angeles and the 2008 Games in Beijing have made an operating profit. Every World Cup Finals in that time has made a profit – and then some.

But then we really shouldn't call it a 'profit'. No, the vast sums made from the World Cup Finals are what FIFA prefer to call a 'surplus', the notion being that any revenue generated from the World Cup is eventually ploughed back into the game, be that through other competitions, tournaments or developmental projects around the world.

In fairness, FIFA does have some significant outlay when not tied up with counting all the cash from a World Cup Finals. Almost none of the other international tournaments they organise and promote (capital construction projects, if you like) make money, and the expenses incurred in staging them are sizeable. The Confederations Cup – the World Cup warm-up – in South Africa of 2009, for example, cost FIFA a cool £27.4 million ($44 million) to stage, while the Under-17 World Cup in Nigeria was another £26.8 million ($43 million). The Under-20 World Cup in Egypt cost £13 million ($21 million), the Club World Cup in the UAE £18.7 million ($30 million) and it cost another £32 million ($51 million) to put on the Women's World Cup in 2011.[9]

While for the most part these tournaments are high-profile events, none generate anything approaching the revenues of the World Cup Finals. At South Africa 2010, for instance, the TV and transmission rights alone sold for nearly £1.5 billion ($2.4 billion), while monies from partners, sponsors and supporters topped £623 million ($1 billion) for the very first time. But then everywhere you look, the revenues from the World Cup are staggering. Hospitality rights bring in £75 million ($120 million), licensing rights are worth £44 million ($71 million) and brand licensing brings in an additional £23 million ($37 million).[10] In all, FIFA took almost £2.5 billion ($4 billion) from their first World Cup venture into Africa and they have already sold £335 million ($539 million) worth of TV rights and £237 million ($381 million) of marketing rights for the next FIFA World Cup Finals to be held in Brazil in 2014. And to think that they gave away the broadcasting rights for nothing at all at the 1954 Finals in Switzerland.

But it's not just FIFA that profits from the World Cup Finals. The host country, for example, also benefits hugely. For a country like South Africa, a nation with a widening disparity between rich and poor[11], the 2010 tournament provided a much-needed fillip for their economy and this despite an initial state outlay of some £1.5 billion ($2.4 billion) to cover the costs of stadia, transport infrastructure, security and the like.[12] Key here is FIFA's subsidy. In contributing around £623 million ($1 billion) to the costs incurred in staging the event – *their* event – FIFA retains all the commercial rights, thereby guaranteeing that their investment makes a significant return. South Africa, meanwhile, was able to enjoy their month in the world sports spotlight. Come the end of the tournament, the event had generated some £2.9 billion ($4.7 billion) of direct expenditure and a total GDP impact of £4.86 billion ($7.8 billion). Moreover, some 415,000 jobs had been created and half a million visitors had come to the country, bringing their wallets with them.[13] It's fair to say that it was one of the nation's most successful months.

The financial benefits of the World Cup Finals are felt everywhere, more so if you happen to be one of the competing nations. Despite a disappointing performance and exit in the second round, England's showing in South Africa, for example, was worth around £1.25 billion ($2 billion) to the UK economy as fans stocked up on beer, snacks, shirts and big screen televisions. And yet it might have been more: had England made it to the final, it's estimated that the economic boon could have been as high as £3 billion ($4.8 billion).[14] Which, presumably, is why the England manager gets so much grief.

Yet the size of FIFA 'the country', both in terms of its constituency and its apparent financial might, is not reflected in economic output, or, to put it another way, potential Gross Domestic Product (GDP). Though a non-profit making organisation, FIFA does publish its accounts and in the annual report of 2011 boasted revenues of £810 million ($1.3 billion), a figure that included a surplus, or profit, of £22.5 million ($36 million). Were these revenues applied to traditional methods of calculating GDP, this would give FIFA a GDP per capita of just £3 ($4.83), placing it at the very foot of the global league table and some way behind the next placed nation, the Democratic Republic of Congo.[15] If FIFA were to achieve an equivalent GDP of a country with a similar population, eg Indonesia, it would have to raise annual revenues by around 1,000 times their existing intake[16], which, given its current business model, would mean staging around 250 FIFA World Cup Finals each year, or one every 1.4 days rather than every four years.

Politically, FIFA at least maintains some notion of democracy, although unlike in a modern democracy, FIFA-registered players – the would-be electorate – do not receive a vote. Under their leader, Sepp Blatter, presidential elections are held every four years while major decisions, such as choosing the president and future host nation of a FIFA World Cup Finals tournament, are voted on by an executive committee of 24 members (its cabinet) drawn from around the world, all of whom are male. Contrast that with, say, the Cabinet in the UK, where women are under-represented but there are nonetheless four female ministers with portfolio sitting. In other words, FIFA is part oligarchy and, given the wealth of some of the executive committee's members, part plutocracy.

In 2007, FIFA officially opened its new headquarters (or parliament) in Zurich. The building, known as the 'Home of FIFA', was designed by acclaimed Swiss architect Tilla Theus and took three years and £99 million ($159 million) to complete. It features five underground levels, a fitness centre, meditation room, geographically-themed parks and a full-size international

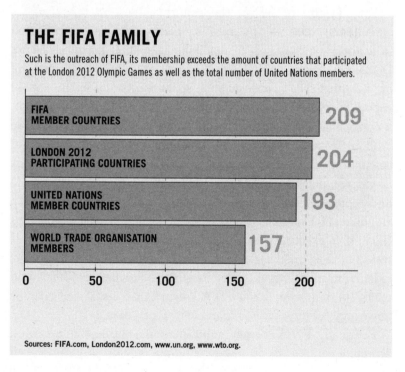

THE FIFA FAMILY

Such is the outreach of FIFA, its membership exceeds the amount of countries that participated at the London 2012 Olympic Games as well as the total number of United Nations members.

FIFA MEMBER COUNTRIES	209
LONDON 2012 PARTICIPATING COUNTRIES	204
UNITED NATIONS MEMBER COUNTRIES	193
WORLD TRADE ORGANISATION MEMBERS	157

0   50   100   150   200

Sources: FIFA.com, London2012.com, www.un.org, www.wto.org.

football pitch.[17] Contrast that with the construction of another new parliament building, the Scottish Parliament at Holyrood, Edinburgh, which was opened three years later than planned (in 2004) and at a final cost of £414.4 million ($667 million) (more than 10 times over the original budget).[18]

And it doesn't even have a football pitch.

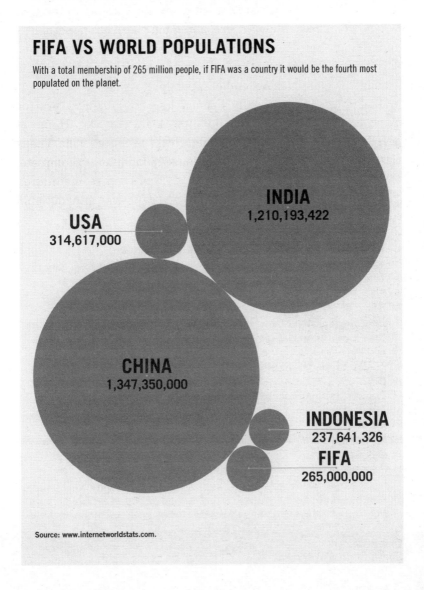

FIFA VS WORLD POPULATIONS

With a total membership of 265 million people, if FIFA was a country it would be the fourth most populated on the planet.

INDIA
1,210,193,422

USA
314,617,000

CHINA
1,347,350,000

INDONESIA
237,641,326

FIFA
265,000,000

Source: www.internetworldstats.com.

NOTES & SOURCES

1. *These are Monaco, Vatican City, Micronesia, the Marshall Islands, Kiribati, Tuvalu, Palau and Nauru.*

2. *FIFA Big Count survey, 2006.*

3. Civil Service Statistics, *Office for National Statistics, 2011. As at 31 March, 2011, Civil Service employment stood at 498,433. This excludes 15,000 people temporarily employed for the 2011 Census.*

4. *'World Cup: To tax or not to tax', Ian Pollock, May 11, 2010 (www.bbc.co.uk/news/10091277).*

5. *FIFA Financial Report, 2010.*

6. *Ibid.*

7. *Ibid.*

8. *International Olympic Committee Estimation, August 7, 2012. This figure is an estimate due to the varying systems used by different countries. Indeed, only 80 out of 200 nations actually use measuring systems.*

9. *FIFA Financial Report, 2010.*

10. *Ibid.*

11. Trends in South African income distribution and poverty since the fall of Apartheid, *Organisation for Economic Co-operation and Development (OECD) Report, 2010.*

12. *FIFA World Cup 2012 Financial Report, Grant Thornton UK LLP.*

13. *Ibid.*

14. *Centre for Retail Research survey, August 2010.*

15. *In 2011, Congo's GDP per capita was estimated by the International Monetary Fund as being £135 ($217).*

16. *In 2011, Indonesia's GDP was estimated by the International Monetary Fund as being £700 billion ($1,127 trillion), placing them 15th in the world.*

17. *www.fifa.com.*

18. *www.scottish.parliament.uk.*

15. WHAT IF YOUR FAMILY CAR WAS A FORMULA 1 RACER?

Guaranteed to get you anywhere in a hurry, but astronomical running costs and very little space to store your shopping

In 1985, *The Economist* magazine estimated that there were some 375 million passenger cars on the world's roads. Today, a little over a quarter of a century later, there are over 1 billion on the planet.[1] Whether it's cut-price bangers or stylish saloons, the world's love affair with the motor car shows no sign of abating. It's a similar story with Formula 1. Now in its 63rd season, the motor racing circuit is proving more popular than ever, with new races added all the time and each Grand Prix broadcast to 187 countries. Cumulative television viewing figures for F1 now exceed 500 million each season.[2]

Whether it's the speed of the cars, the engines' roar or the smell of the pit lane, the allure of the Formula 1 circus remains undeniably potent. Perhaps it's the fact that many F1 fans would like nothing better than to swap places with Sebastian Vettel or Fernando Alonso for a day, even if it was just for one lap. The truth of the matter, though, is that while the F1 car is exactly the sort of eminently desirable vehicle that many drivers would love to have sitting in their garage, it's not only extremely impractical as a runaround but also eye-wateringly expensive.

Of course, in terms of design and performance the modern Formula 1 racing car is a piece of precision engineering unmatched in mainstream sport. Here, after all, is a vehicle where the steering wheel alone boasts 23 dials and buttons (not one of which controls the volume on the radio), over 120 different functions and where you won't get much change from £20,000 ($32,000), should you wish to buy one.[3] Despite weighing only 2.8 lbs (1.3 kg), the wheel gives the driver the ability to do everything from changing gears to applying the rev. limiter and adjusting the fuel/air mix to altering the brake pressure. An LCD screen meanwhile provides vital data, such as speed and lap times. In the latter respect, the screen on the F1 steering wheel is not dissimilar to the displays in some of the dashboards of modern cars. What does differ, however, is just about everything else.

Certainly, the F1 car is a serious piece of kit. Each member of a Formula 1 team, for example, will get through an average of eight engines per season per car. That's an entirely new engine, incidentally, not one that's been patched up to get through the MOT or annual motor inspection. The gearbox, meanwhile, contains software so complex that it can change gears in less than 0.01 seconds, or 50 times faster than it takes a human to blink. Obviously, while that split-second timing is crucial on the racetrack, it's not so essential when you're sitting in traffic, waiting for the lights to change. Indeed, the telemetry technology used in F1 cars means that you can also track and locate virtually everything that's happening to your car during the race and, more importantly, what's going wrong with it, from drops in tyre pressure to changes in the engine's output.

But there's a long way to go before you actually get to sit in your own F1 car, not least locating it in the first place. Most manufacturers prefer not to sell their old or historic vehicles on the open market. McLaren, for instance, gives used stock to their showrooms, use it for promotional purposes or simply keep it in storage; Ferrari, on the other hand, actively promotes sales of used cars. If you've got the wherewithal, you might find yourself invited to their iconic HQ at Maranello, near Bologna in northern Italy, where you can peruse the cars on offer in their F1 department, which usually has around 60 vehicles in stock at any given time. Expect competition from

A-list celebrities and sports stars, plus a price tag of at least £623,000 ($1 million).

The beauty of the Ferrari F1 car is that it doesn't suffer the same kind of depreciation in value as the Ford Focus. Drive a new Focus off the forecourt and within a year it will have lost 60 per cent of its value.[4] Pick up a Ferrari F1 car and it will hold its value in perpetuity, provided the vehicle is kept in good condition. In 2011, for example, the 2006 Ferrari 248 F1 racer driven by Felipe Massa in the 2006 Grand Prix season (and the same car that won seven of the last nine races) was listed for sale on the online luxury marketplace JamesList for £1.87 million ($3 million).

While Ferraris have their own special place in the hearts and minds of petrolheads, other F1 cars can be picked up for a fraction of the price. An Arrows 2001 AX3, converted to take two passengers as well as the driver, can be yours for just £299,500 ($482,195), while a 1998 Jordan EJ198, as driven by Damon Hill and Ralf Schumacher, was available for sale for just £59,995 ($96,591).[5] A 1998 Ford Focus, the year the car was introduced, will set you back around £300 ($483).

If the initial price tag doesn't dissuade you, then the running costs might and if you compare it to the average family car you'll begin to appreciate just how costly an F1 car is to run. In the UK, the country's best-selling family car is the Ford Focus[6], which costs £13,995 ($22,531) on the road.[7] The average Formula 1 car, excluding the many millions ploughed into research and testing, is approximately £2 million ($3.2 million).[8]

The good news is that F1 cars use petrol very similar to that used in the Ford Focus (albeit with a more tightly controlled mix). But the bad news is that they only do around 4.5 miles (7.2 kilometres) per gallon, making the average journey of seven miles (11 kilometres)[9] cost £6.85 ($11.03) at current prices, as opposed to the 72p ($1.16) that it would cost in petrol[10] to make the journey in an entry level 1.6 Ford Focus Duratec. For the average British family which travels 8,430 miles (13,567 kilometres) each year[11] in their Focus, the total cost of fuel would be £868 ($1,396). If they were to use a Formula 1 car instead, however, they would be faced with a bill of £8252 ($13,286).

But what if you wanted to holiday in your car, maybe take a road trip? How about the world-famous Route 66, for example? Stretching from Chicago, Illinois to Santa Monica, California, the 2,451 miles (3,944 kilometres) of this fabled path ordinarily takes four to five days of solid driving to complete, longer if you take it easy and stop off along the way. Do it in an F1 car, however, and if you maintain a top speed of 229.8mph (369.8kph)[12], and if you share the driving, you could complete the journey in a little over 10.5 hours. But while it's quicker to complete, the trip would also be significantly cheaper than taking a journey of similar length in the UK or continental Europe. With petrol in the US currently at $3.81 (£2.37) a gallon[13], the total cost of fuel for the journey would be $2,075.17 (around £1,286).

But it's not just the fuel costs that are crippling. Take the Focus and you'll spend an average of £6,689 ($10,769) per year running and maintaining it[14,] and while an F1 car could be made road-legal (although kerbs and road humps may represent a problem), getting insurance might prove to be an insurmountable problem. According to Direct Line, one of the UK's leading car insurers, a male driver, aged 40, with a clean driving licence, in a professional job and with a garage to house the car, could expect to pay a premium of £250,000 ($400,000) per annum for his F1 runaround.[15]

Run into some mechanical problems with an F1 car, however, and you may well need to seek assistance from the IMF. A new engine, for example, will set you back £148,860 ($239,664) (it has over 1,000 parts that take 80 hours to assemble) and a replacement gearbox costs £89,330 ($143,821). A single tyre, meanwhile, is around £450 ($724) and if someone dents the front wing when you're parked at Sainsbury's supermarket, it'll be £14,934 ($24,043) to replace it. In total, it's estimated that it will cost you £4.76 million ($7.66 million) to own and run an F1 car for a lifetime[16] – and it doesn't even have its own CD player.

ULTIMATE FORMULA ONE ROAD TRIPS

The costs and time of taking a F1 car for a spin on these famous and infamous journeys.

Berliner Ring (Berlin, Germany)

Distance: 112 miles

Estimated time taken in a modern F1 car*

46 mins

Cost in petrol (UK January 2013)**

£110

M25 (London, England)

Distance: 117 miles

Estimated time taken in a modern F1 car*

48 mins

Cost in petrol (UK January 2013)**

£114

Eyre Highway (Australia)

Distance: 1,041 miles

Estimated time taken in a modern F1 car*

7 hrs, 11 mins

Cost in petrol (UK January 2013)**

£1,019

Route 66 (North America)

Distance: 2,448 miles

Estimated time taken in a modern F1 car*

16 hrs, 52 mins

Cost in petrol (UK January 2013)**

£2,396

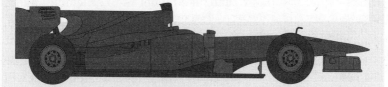

* Based on Fernando Alonso's Silverstone 2010 British Grand Prix lap record, with an average speed of 145.01 mph (233.373 kph). Source: www.silverstone.co.uk
** prices based on 4.5 miles per gallon. Source: www.fuel-economy.co.uk

COVER ME! THE COST OF INSURING YOUR F1 CAR

The financially savvy motorist is always on the lookout for the best possible deal when it comes to getting vehichle cover. But the best deal you can get to insure you and your F1 car is unlikely to bring a smile to your face. According to Direct Line insurance, a 40-year-old male or female driver with a clean driving history, a maximum No Claims Discount and having held a full license for over five years would be facing an annual bill of £250,000 ($400,000) to insure their F1 car with an excess of £25,000 ($40,000) for any claims made.

There is, moreover, a raft of restrictions and exclusion clauses attached to any potential policy. The car, for example, must be kept in a garage and fitted with a tracker while breakdown cover would not be included in the policy because of the specialist nature of the vehicle. You won't get a courtesy car either as it may be a little tricky getting a similarly equipped vehicle from a supplier.[15]

NOTES & SOURCES

1. *A report in August 2011 by Ward's Auto – 'The Information Center For And About The Global Auto Industry' – calculated that there were 1.015 billion cars on the world's roads.*
2. *Formula One Management (FOM) Report, January 2010.*
3. *Bleacher Report, Formula One: 'Money, Money, Money, Component Costs', July 2008.*
4. *Wisebuyers.com, August 2012.*
5. *F1Sales.com, August 2012.*
6. *Society of Motor Manufacturers and Traders (SMMT) Report, 2011. New registrations for the Focus totalled 81,832; only the smaller Ford Fiesta sold more.*
7. *www.ford.co.uk, July 18, 2012.*
8. *Bleacher Report, Formula One: 'Money, Money, Money, Component Costs', July 2008.*
9. *Department for Transport National Travel Survey, 2010.*
10. *Average price of unleaded petrol in the UK, www.petrolprices.com, July 18, 2012.*
11. *Department for Transport National Travel Survey, 2010.*
12. *Achieved by Antônio Pizzonia of the BMW Williams F1 team in the Italian Grand Prix, 2004.*
13. *American Automobile Association, Daily Fuel Gauge, October 6, 2012.*
14. *RAC Report, November 2011.*
15. *Dave Meader, Head of Technical Underwriting, Direct Line car insurance, December 2012.*

16. YOU'RE BETTER OFF IN THE COMMENTARY BOX
Why Alan Hansen is more valuable than the US President

Superficially at least, being a sports analyst appears to be one of the easier jobs within sport. Free from the concomitant pressures of performing on the pitch or the many stresses of coaching, pundits can enjoy a relatively comfortable life, espousing their expert views to the watching world and, in many cases, commanding the kind of remuneration that dwarfs that of many of their contemporaries who are still actively involved in the playing of the game itself.

For many sports stars, the choice of whether to opt for the comfort of the television studio is an easy decision, especially for those players who are articulate and charismatic. But it's a competitive world and one where only the very best, in theory, are paid the kind of sky-high salaries that eclipse those on the field of play. The BBC's Alan Hansen, for example, was until recently paid £1.5 million ($2.4 million) a year for his weekly appearance on their flagship football show, *Match of the Day*, a figure that works out at around £40,000 ($64,000) per 90-minute show.[1]

While Hansen's pay packet was more than the average wage of a Premier League footballer – in 2011, that stood at £22,353 ($35,988) a week, or £1.16 million ($1.86 million) a year[2] – the sheer scale of his wages, especially in a time of austerity, has rankled with the ordinary man and woman in the street. It's easy to see why. The starting salary for a registered nurse in the UK, for instance, is just £21,176 ($34,093)[3], while a secondary school teacher starts his or her career on a little over £400 ($640) more per year.[4] That, put simply, means you could have 70 extra nurses or teachers for just one Alan Hansen. Alternatively, how about 14 extra GPs[5], or 8.6 High Court judges[6]?

Some of the most powerful people in the world cannot hold a candle to Hansen. The Russian President, Vladimir Putin, for example, has an official salary of just £72,000 ($115,000)[7], while the British Prime Minister, David Cameron, earns £142,500 ($229,000)[8] – about a tenth of Hansen's wage – for running the United Kingdom. Across the Pond, his opposite number and arguably the most powerful man on the planet, US President Barack Obama, receives $400,000 per annum (around £250,000).[9] Even the best paid politician in the G20, Australian Prime Minister Julia Gillard, earns just a fifth of Hansen's remuneration.[10]

That said, the BBC recently announced that Hansen, along with fellow *Match of the Day* analysts Alan Shearer, Mark Lawrenson and Lee Dixon (who has since moved to ITV Sport) would all be taking pay cuts as part of a cost-cutting exercise at the Corporation. The programme's anchor, former England international Gary Lineker, is also expected to take a reduction in his reported £2 million ($3.2 million) -a-year salary when his contract comes up for renewal in August 2013.

When the story of Hansen's salary at the BBC came to light, it provoked consternation among football fans, not least because the presenter was not particularly known for his contentious or strident opinions. Indeed, such was the furore that it even raised eyebrows in Parliament, with Damian Collins, a Conservative member of the Culture, Media and Sport select committee, asking the BBC to justify why they paid Hansen such a large amount. "It is a lot of money for Alan Hansen, and the BBC needs to justify such large amounts at a time when every pound they spend is being scrutinised," he declared.[11] Collins had a point. After all, Hansen's salary was effectively being paid for out of public money, and amounted to the full annual television licence fee of over 10,309 BBC viewers.[12] That's like everyone at an average Barnsley FC home game all handing over £145.50 ($234) each – straight to Alan Hansen[13].

What the revelations did demonstrate, however, was that for the most part, an analyst's worth is based not on what he says but rather on the success, profile and reputation he enjoyed during his playing career. In the case of Hansen it was his career in club football that gave him his opportunity, not his 26 caps for Scotland. As one of the stalwart defenders in Liverpool's all-conquering side of the late 1970s and 1980s, winning eight League titles, three European Cups, two FA Cups and four League Cups, he was widely tipped as a future Liverpool manager but opted instead for the relative safety of the TV studio sofa. It's entirely understandable: for one, you don't get any of the pressure that comes hand-in-hand with the role of football manager and, quite often, it's actually more lucrative to become a pundit.

Look at the example of Hansen's *Match of the Day* colleague Alan Shearer, who took over at his old club, Newcastle United, at the tail end of the 2008–09 season despite never having coached a club before in his life. At the time it seemed like a good idea – the Magpies were eight games away from being relegated and here was one of the club's most legendary players stepping in to save them from impending doom. The result? Just one win, two draws and five defeats, and Newcastle United dropped into the Championship. Shearer, meanwhile, went back to the warmth of the *Match of the Day* studio.

Shearer was lucky in that he landed one of the top jobs in British football punditry as soon as he had retired from playing. For most analysts, though, there's a clear pecking order, especially in football, not to mention a huge disparity across sports in the money they can expect to receive. And while you may assume soccer, or rather the cash-rich English Premier League, is the best paid of all televised sport, there are some other sports whose pundits also enjoy a bumper pay day. In tennis, for example, the seven-times Grand Slam title winner John McEnroe commanded a fee of £10,000 ($16,000) per day for commentating for the BBC during the fortnight of the 2011 Wimbledon Championships. Meanwhile, his doubles partner (with whom he had won 50 doubles titles), Peter Fleming, was offered around £10,000 ($16,000) for the entire two weeks by the BBC, an offer he subsequently declined.[14]

Like tennis, golf can also be a lucrative sport, especially for those players whose career records stands comparison with the very best. Great Britain's six-time major winner Nick Faldo, for example, has a contract worth a reported £8 million ($12.8 million) a year with the American broadcaster CBS to cover the PGA Tour.[15] To put that into context, only the world's number-one ranked player, Northern Ireland's Rory McIlroy, and the American Brandt Snedeker, who secured the £10 million ($16 million) bonus on offer for winning the season-ending FedEx Cup, earned more prize-money in 2012 than Faldo received in the commentary box.[16]

But when it comes to commentary, does Faldo have the X factor? Perhaps he does. Before the 2012 Ryder Cup at the Medinah Country Club, for instance, he had predicted that the biennial match between the US and Europe would end in a tie – something that had only happened twice in 38 matches. At the time his opinion was widely seen as a fence-sitting exercise designed to keep both sides of the Atlantic happy. Come the end of the epic encounter, though, and Faldo's forecast was almost spot on and but for an extremely missable putt that America's Tiger Woods conceded to Europe's Francesco Molinari on the very last hole of the tournament, it was a prophecy that would have come to pass.

The United States of America, then, is where the money is for any aspiring pundit. Across all sports the salaries on offer for talented commentators are staggering. While the likes of American football's Dan Marino (CBS) and basketball's Charles Barkley (TNT) can command multi-million wage packets, they do so because (a) they reached the very pinnacle of their sport, and (b) their work spans an entire season. Those athletes and former athletes called upon to work on less popular sports in more limited time spans obviously earn significantly less.

It's the same in the United Kingdom. For every Alan Hansen, there's another former professional being paid a couple of hundred pounds for a radio commentary, less if it's just local radio. It's a tough life for those not at the top so when the opportunity to

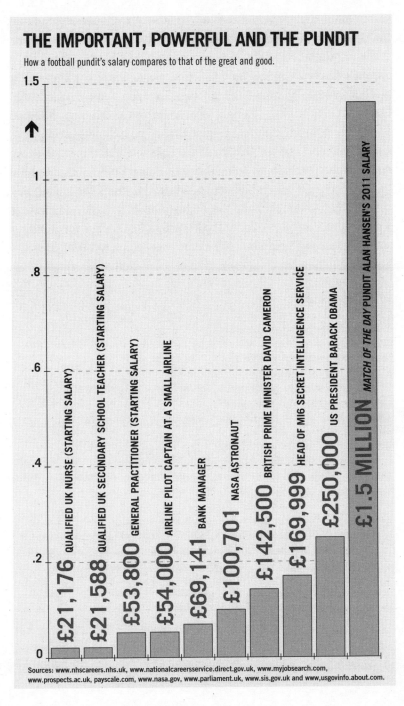

THE IMPORTANT, POWERFUL AND THE PUNDIT

How a football pundit's salary compares to that of the great and good.

1.5

1

.8

.6

.4

.2

0

£21,176 QUALIFIED UK NURSE (STARTING SALARY)

£21,588 QUALIFIED UK SECONDARY SCHOOL TEACHER (STARTING SALARY)

£53,800 GENERAL PRACTITIONER (STARTING SALARY)

£54,000 AIRLINE PILOT CAPTAIN AT A SMALL AIRLINE

£69,141 BANK MANAGER

£100,701 NASA ASTRONAUT

£142,500 BRITISH PRIME MINISTER DAVID CAMERON

£169,999 HEAD OF MI6 SECRET INTELLIGENCE SERVICE

£250,000 US PRESIDENT BARACK OBAMA

£1.5 MILLION *MATCH OF THE DAY PUNDIT ALAN HANSEN'S 2011 SALARY*

Sources: www.nhscareers.nhs.uk, www.nationalcareersservice.direct.gov.uk, www.myjobsearch.com, www.prospects.ac.uk, payscale.com, www.nasa.gov, www.parliament.uk, www.sis.gov.uk and www.usgovinfo.about.com.

supplement their salary comes along, it's entirely understandable that they may wish to grab it. In the UK, at least, that often means throwing themselves at the mercy of 'reality TV' with the BBC's *Strictly Come Dancing* now the first port of call for the young pundit keen to increase his profile. To date, former cricketers Darren Gough, Phil Tufnell, Mark Ramprakash and Michael Vaughan, retired athletes Roger Black and Denise Lewis, ex-rugby players Martin Offiah, Matt Dawson and Austin Healey and former footballers John Barnes, Peter Shilton and Robbie Savage have all taken part in the show, juggling their analyst's roles with the demands of the dancefloor. It's hardly surprising when there's a cheque for £50,000 ($80,000) on offer for donning the fake tan and sequins.[17] Which of course is what Alan Hansen gets for doing a little over one edition of *Match of the Day*.

NOTES & SOURCES

1 & 11. *'Alan Hansen Takes Home £40,000 ($64,044) Per Match of the Day Appearance'*, Metro, October 30, 2011.

2. *'Exclusive: Official Figures Show Top-flight Wages Are Now FIVE Times More Than in Championship'*, Mail On Sunday, October 29, 2011.

3. *Royal College of Nursing, NHS Agenda for Change Pay Scales 2012/13.*

4. *A secondary school teacher's starting salary in the UK is £21,588 ($34,756) (Nationalcareersservice.direct.gov.uk).*

5. *'GPs Take Home £100,000 ($161,000) Average Salary Despite Pay Fall'*, Times, September 27, 2012.

6. *High Court Judges earn £172,753 ($278,123) per annum (www.justice.gov.uk/downloads/publications/corporate-reports/MoJ/2012/judicial-salaries-2012-13.pdf).*

7. *'How Did Vladimir Putin Afford His £450,000 ($724,000) Watch Collection Worth Six Times His Annual Salary?'*, Daily Mail, June 9, 2012.

8. *www.parliament.uk/about/faqs.*

9. *106th Congress Public Law 58, Treasury and General Government Appropriations Act, 2000.*

10. *Australian PM Julia Gillard earns A$481,000, or around £318,582 per annum ('Anger Over MPs' Pay Rise'*, Sydney Morning Herald, July 4, 2012.

12. *The cost of a one-year television licence in the UK is £145.50 ($234).*

13. *Barnsley FC's average home attendance in the Football League Championship of 2011–12 was 10,332 (www.football-league.co.uk).*

14. *www.dailymail.co.uk/sport/tennis/article-2007540/Charles-Sale-John-McEnroes-BBC-pay-aces-Peter-Fleming.html.*

15. *www.dailymail.co.uk/sport/othersports/article-408897/Nick-Faldos-8m-US-television-smile.*

16. *2012 PGA Tour Total Money (Official and Unofficial) – www.pgatour.com.*

17. *'Robbie Savage to Dance on Strictly'*, Sun, September 5, 2011.

17. FASTBALLS AND LIGHTNING STRIKES
What's the fastest ball sport?

In sport, where for the most part hand-eye coordination is key, the ability to react quickly often means the difference between defeat or victory, agony or ecstasy. Certainly in mainstream ball sports where players are pitted against each other, the increasing emphasis on power has proved to be one of the most effective ways of improving the chances of success, not least because it can reduce the time in which the opposition has to react to any given situation.[1]

In some sports, like cricket and baseball, it's rare for the ball to be bowled or pitched in excess of 100mph. In cricket, for example, pace bowlers typically bowl at speeds of between 85 and 95mph and only two players to have broken the 100mph barrier, Australia's Shaun Tait and the fastest of them all, Pakistan's Shoaib Akhtar, who delivered a ball at 100.2mph in the ICC Cricket World Cup in South Africa of 2003. Remarkably, the batsman on the receiving end (England's Nick Knight) not only got a bat on the ball but succeeded in steering it away to safety on to the leg side.[2]

The 100mph pitch in baseball is more common. Since speed radar guns were introduced in the 1980s, there have been many examples of pitchers throwing fastballs in excess of the magical mark and up until September 24, 2010, the fastest recorded pitch belonged to Joel Zumaya of the Detroit Tigers, who clocked up an amazing 104.8mph in a play-off in October 2006. It was then that the Cincinnati Reds' Cuban pitcher Aroldis Chapman hurled one down to the San Diego Padres' Tony Gwynn at an astonishing 105mph. "I didn't see it until the ball was behind me," Gwynn later admitted. "I was trying not to look at the radar reading because I'd be intimidated."[3]

Gwynn's incredulity typifies those who find themselves on the wrong end of a fastball. In baseball and cricket, studies have shown just how little time the batsman has to react to a fast delivery. For a delivery of 90mph on a standard length cricket pitch of 22 yards (20 metres), he has around half a second to react. In that time he will establish the correct trajectory of the ball, decide which shot to play and then execute his chosen shot. And in both cricket and baseball, batsmen must also allow for variables such as the ball swinging in the air, or (as happens in cricket), the ball hitting the ground and then deviating from the course one would ordinarily expect it to follow.[4]

Russia's Denis Kulyash is capable of propelling a hockey puck at speeds of 110.3mph, it's not dissimilar to standing in a firing line – which goes a long way toward explaining why the players need so much protective clothing.

A similar problem faces goalkeepers in ice hockey. With a regulation puck weighing between 5.5 and 6 oz (156–170 grams) and players such as Russia's Denis Kulyash capable of propelling it at speeds of 110.3mph[5], it's not dissimilar to standing in a firing line – which goes a long way toward explaining why the players need so much protective clothing.

It's extremely rare for a football to be struck at such speeds – with one notable exception. In November 2006, Sporting Lisbon's Brazilian fullback Ronny Heberson Furtado de Araújo (known simply as 'Ronny') scored a memorable free-kick against Naval that was clocked at 131.82mph.[6] Television footage of the goal is remarkable – you can't even see the ball in flight. One moment Ronny steps up to strike the ball, and in the blink of an eye the goalkeeper is picking the ball out of the net. What made the shot all the more remarkable was not that it eclipsed the shot believed to be the game's previous best – a 114mph humdinger by Sheffield Wednesday's David Hirst against Arsenal in 1996 – but that it did so by nearly 18mph.

But such power pales into insignificance compared to the speeds generated in some of the racquet sports. In tennis, for example, players in the men's game routinely serve in excess of 135mph but in May 2012 the Australian professional Sam Groth hit the quickest-recorded serve in history when he bludgeoned a 163.4mph ace during a Challenger tournament in Busan in South Korea. Groth, ranked 340th in the world at the time, also had serves of 157.5 and 158.9mph during the match, both of which were faster than the previous record of 156mph, set by Croatia's Ivo Karlovic in a Davis Cup tie against Germany in March 2011. Despite this, Groth still went down to Uladzimir Ignatik of Belarus in straight sets.[7]

Of course, the power generated by tennis players' serves is largely attributable not just to the speed of the racquet face on impact, but also to the weight of the racquet itself, the stiffness of the frame and the tension of the string bed; composition and age of the ball are also key. A regulation tennis ball should measure between 65.4–68.6 mm and weigh between 56 and 59.4g[8] and, like a cricket ball, it will travel faster when newer. Conversely, in a sport such as table tennis (ping pong), where the 40 mm-diameter ball weighs just 2.7 g[9], the air friction impacted on it means that even the hardest shots rarely reach speeds of over 60mph.[10]

But it's not the machismo of men's tennis that takes the plaudits as the fastest ball sport or, to be more accurate, the fastest sport where a projectile is propelled. No, that honour goes to badminton, a game where the explosive power on display often goes unnoticed. Though the presence of feathers on the shuttlecock (and the subsequent drag imparted) means

SPORTS SPEED THRILLS

Speeds in sport are increasing, and badminton leads the way with 250+ mph exchanges.

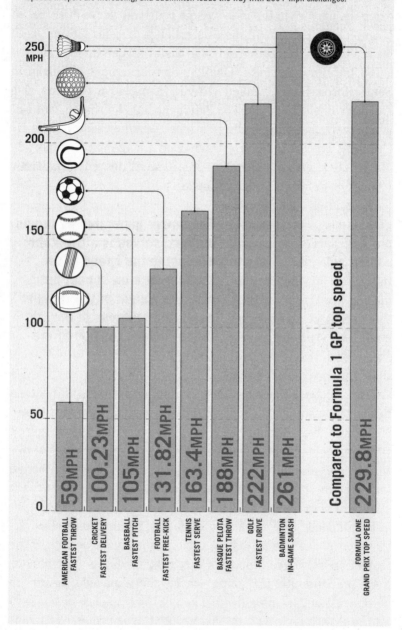

250 MPH

200

150

100

50

0

| 59MPH | 100.23MPH | 105MPH | 131.82MPH | 163.4MPH | 188MPH | 222MPH | 261MPH |

AMERICAN FOOTBALL FASTEST THROW

CRICKET FASTEST DELIVERY

BASEBALL FASTEST PITCH

FOOTBALL FASTEST FREE-KICK

TENNIS FASTEST SERVE

BASQUE PELOTA FASTEST THROW

GOLF FASTEST DRIVE

BADMINTON IN-GAME SMASH

Compared to Formula 1 GP top speed

229.8MPH

FORMULA ONE GRAND PRIX TOP SPEED

that it decelerates much faster than a ball, the aerodynamics are such that top players can typically hit it at speeds of over 180mph, although the fastest-recorded hit in a competitive match, recognised by *Guinness World Records*, was measured at 206mph.[11] However, in a test carried out by the racquet manufacturer Yonex in Tokyo, Japan of 2009, the Malaysian player Tan Boon Heong struck a shuttlecock that flew through the air at a staggering 261.5mph. Or, to put it another way, about six times faster than the goose providing the feathers for the shuttlecock.[12]

NOTES & SOURCES

1. *Golf, where the American long driver Jason Zuback has propelled a golf ball at a record speed of 222mph, is not included as the ball is stationary when struck.*
2. *The fastest delivery in international cricket is 100.23mph by Shoaib Akhtar (Pakistan) versus England in the 2003 ICC Cricket World Cup, Newlands, Cape Town, South Africa.*
3. *'Chapman throws fastest pitch ever recorded',* Steve Henson, Yahoo! Sports, Saturday, September 25, 2010.
4. *'From eye movements to actions: how batsmen hit the ball',* Michael F. Land and Peter McLeod, Nature Neuroscience, *1340–45 (2000).*
5. *Denis Kulyash set the world record of 110.3mph during the KHL All-Star Superskills Competition of February 2011.*
6. *Portuguese First Division match, Figueira da Foz, November 26, 2006.*
7. *www.atpworldtour.com/News/Tennis/2012/05/Features/Groth-Fast-Serve.aspx.*
8. *International Tennis Federation, www.itftennis.com/media/118889/118889.pdf*
9. *ITTF Technical Leaflet 'T3: The Ball', International Table Tennis Federation, December 2009.*
10. *In the International Table Tennis Federation's 'World's fastest Smash' competition of October 2003, New Zealand's Lark Brandt hit a smash at 69.9mph.*
11. *Fu Haifeng of China, 2005 Sudirman Cup held in Beijing, China on May 10–15, 2005 (International Badminton Federation).*
12. *www.badzine.net/news/badminton-in-guinness-book-of-world-records/2378.*

18. BECKONOMICS
Is football's global marketing machine worth all the money?

It all started with a goal from the halfway line at Selhurst Park in August 1996, a sweetly struck shot that sailed over the Wimbledon goalkeeper Neil Sullivan and launched a professional career that would come to dominate domestic and international football – and far beyond – for a generation.

Now approaching 40, David Beckham has enjoyed a career that has come to define the modern age of professional football. He is, arguably, the man who helped to turn footballers into global superstars and the man who, more than any other player of his era, played a key role in ushering in a new age of opportunity and prosperity for professional players. As the playing career of the former England captain nears its end, it's clear that his influence has gone way beyond the confines of the football pitch. From celebrity magazines and tabloids to his management at 19 Entertainment, from innumerable global brands to the clubs he has played for, myriad people and organisations have benefited from Beckham's worldwide popularity.

Beckham's career path in professional football has resembled an unstoppable juggernaut. From humble beginnings in the East End of London, he has been a model of professionalism on the pitch and a marketing man's dream away from it, a heady mix that has seen him become the most high-profile and richest footballer in the world, even though he was never once voted FIFA's World Player of the Year.

It was at his first club, Manchester United, that Beckham's celebrity and, crucially, his vast earning potential first became evident, not least because his position as one of United's most influential players had not only gained him international recognition but also won him the England captaincy. The fact that he was married to a Spice Girl as well merely served to enhance his (and her) celebrity still further.

Certainly, Manchester United realised the marketability of their matinee idol midfielder and when they offered him a new contract in 2002, for around £90,000 ($145,000) a week, it was the first time that a proportion of such a deal included recompense for a player's 'image rights', the idea being that as Manchester United would also benefit financially from using Beckham's name and image in their merchandise and marketing campaigns, the player, by now a household name, should also benefit. It was a canny move on the part of Beckham and his advisers and the new contract – £70,000 (£112,000) a week in basic pay and £20,000 ($32,000) a week for image rights – represented a huge 300 per cent increase on his previous deal at Old Trafford.

Indeed, it has always been Beckham's marketability that has made him such an attractive proposition for clubs around the world. Even as his powers on the pitch have waned there are still clubs, like the Italian giants AC Milan, who are willing to take him on, safe in the knowledge that any investment they do make will be more than paid back. For the most part, it doesn't even seem to matter if the impact he makes on the pitch is that significant. The simple fact that he is at the club is enough to get everyone, from the fans to the accountants, genuinely excited.

Throughout his career, Beckham has proved to be a marketing machine *par excellence*, both on the field and off it. With good looks, charm, talent in abundance and fashion icon status, he has proved to be an irresistible proposition to some huge global brands. Vodafone, Diesel, adidas, Pepsi, EA Sports, Marks & Spencer and Motorola have all fallen under Beckham's spell in the last 15 years. The effect he has is startling. When he began modelling men's underwear for Armani in February 2008, for instance, sales of the briefs rose by 150 per cent at Selfridges in

London's Oxford Street, while other leading high street stores such as John Lewis also reported sudden spikes in sales on the back of Beckham's endorsement.[1] Similarly, Proctor & Gamble, parent company of Gillette, recorded a 33 per cent increase in sales in 2006, due in part, to Beckham's endorsement of their new Fusion razor.[2]

And even though he's near the end of his playing career, Beckham's demand as a brand ambassador shows no sign of waning. In 2011, for instance, he still earned many millions from sponsorship deals with companies such as adidas, Samsung and Diet Coke. Accounts filed at Companies House show that Beckham's company, Footwork Productions, took in £15.2 million ($24.4 million) in 2011, of which Beckham paid himself £13.3 million ($21.4 million), or, to break it down, about £36,000 ($58,000) each and every day.

When Beckham left in 2003, Manchester United were the world's biggest club in terms of revenues, while Real Madrid ranked fourth. Four years later, when Beckham left the Bernabéu, Real had usurped United at the top...

And this, it must be remembered, is in addition to his salary at LA Galaxy and the joint earnings he has with his wife Victoria via their fragrance range (a venture for which at launch the pair were paid £8.5 million ($13.7 million) in 2007).

Put simply, Beckham makes money wherever he goes – and not just for 'Brand Beckham'. As you will discover in chapter 22, Beckham's impact on shirt sales at Real Madrid paid off his £24.5 million ($40 million) transfer fee in a matter of months, but his presence at the Bernabéu more generally was seen as the primary driver in the huge increase in merchandise sales at the club, which totalled £377 million ($607 million) over his four years at the club.[3] Interestingly, when Beckham left Old Trafford in 2003, Manchester United were the world's biggest club in terms of revenues, while Real Madrid ranked fourth. Four years later, when Beckham left the Bernabéu, Real had usurped United at the top of the tree.

It was a similar story when Beckham signed a £128 million ($206 million), five-year deal with the Los Angeles Galaxy in the United States Major League Soccer (MLS) in the summer of 2007. Prior to his formal introduction at the club's Home Depot Center stadium (an event attended by 5,000 fans and 700 members of the media), the club had already sold 250,000 team shirts in advance. Yet again, though, his impact began to kick in way before Beckham even pulled on the Galaxy shirt, with the club negotiating a record-breaking five-year £12.5 million ($20 million) shirt sponsorship deal with Herbalife, partly because the nutrition company knew the kind of exposure they would receive once Beckham was wearing the Herbalife-branded Galaxy shirt. At the Home Depot Center, meanwhile, the club immediately sold an additional 11,000 season tickets while all 42 luxury corporate boxes were also snapped up on news of Beckham's transfer.[4]

While the cost of buying a franchise – a sure sign of the profile of the game – is around £26 million ($42 million), four times the price that it was when Beckham joined the League in 2007.

Five years on and Beckham's time in the MLS has come to an end. In November 2012, the 37-year-old midfielder announced that he would be leaving the LA Galaxy at the end of the 2012 MLS season, declaring that he wanted to "experience one last challenge before the end of my playing career", with no fewer than 12 clubs from across the globe making him lucrative offers. He leaves a game that seems finally to be flourishing in the States despite decades of false dawns and stubborn resistance from American sports fans brought up on the traditional diet of baseball, basketball and American football. The average League attendance in the MLS is now up to 18,000 while the cost of buying a franchise – a sure sign of the profile of the game – is around £26 million ($42 million), four times the price that it was when Beckham joined the League in 2007.

Moreover, in 2013 there will be 19 teams in the MLS (five more than 2007), while the quality of the players now making the move to the US is significantly higher than pre-Beckham, with the likes of France's Thierry Henry, Ireland's Robbie Keane and Australia's Tim Cahill all making the move across the Atlantic. This, it could be argued, is entirely down to Beckham's presence in the MLS and the notion that if it's good enough for him, then it must be good enough for pretty much every other player in the game.

Now, as Beckham heads off to a new venture, he can confidently expect not just to enrapture an entirely new market but also to reap the huge rewards that will inevitably go hand in hand with taking Brand Beckham to a whole new territory. Once upon a time, Beckham's wife, Victoria, cheekily called her husband 'Golden Balls'. It's safe to say she had a point.

VEND IT LIKE BECKHAM

The career of the world's most recognisable and marketable footballer in numbers.

5

He is just the fifth player in World Cup history to score twice from a direct free-kick; the other four were Pele, Roberto Rivelino, Teofilo Cubillas and Bernard Genghini.

3

The number of teams with which he has won league titles: Manchester United, Real Madrid and the Los Angeles Galaxy.

6

The number of Premier League titles he won with Manchester United.

20

The approximate number of tattoos on Beckham's body, including jesus being carried by three angels and a tattoo of his wife, Victoria.

32

His ranking on the 2012 Forbes Celebrity 100 List, which ranks the world's most powerful celebrities.

23

His shirt number at Real Madrid and at the Los Angeles Galaxy in admiration for basketball player Michael Jordan, who also wore the number.

35
Forbes lists him as earning £29m in 2012, making him 35th for money on the Forbes Celebrity 100 List and still the highest-paid footballer in the world.

59
The number of times he captained england.

700
The number of accredited media members on July 13, 2007, when Beckham was officially introduced as a Los Angeles Galaxy player.

115
Record number of England caps for an outfield player.10 short of goalkeeper Peter Shilton's record.

£14m
The value of the Beckhams' 13,000-square-foot plot, six-bedroom villa in Beverly Hills.

$3m
His salary at the Los Angeles Galaxy in 2012. Down $2.5m from his first contract.

£377m
According to Forbes, Beckham's five years at Real Madrid were primarily responsible for an increase in merchandise sales, a total reported to top £377m

£190m
According to the *Sunday Times*' Rich List, Beckham's estimated net worth in April 2012

NOTES & SOURCES
1. Daily Telegraph, *July 6, 2008.*
2. *www.bbc.co.uk, October 31, 2006.*
3. *www.forbes.com.*
4. The Beckham Experiment, *Grant Wahl, 2010.*
5. *www.guardian.co.uk/football/2012/may/26/david-beckham-pay-cut-mls.*

19. IQs AND PBs
Does intelligence count for anything in sport?

From uninspiring post-match interviews through to front-page night club antics, footballers rarely do themselves any favours when it comes to countering allegations that they're perhaps not the brightest stars in the sports firmament.

Yet it's an old and largely unfair contention, not least because the intelligence a player shows off the field rarely has anything to do with the ability he displays on it. No, for the most part, the professional footballer's education is not completed in the traditional manner. Their classroom is the changing room, their playground the football pitch, and once they've finished secondary school then, all being well, it's headlong into a long and lucrative career in the professional game where it matters not one jot what grades you got in Geography.

Football differs from many sports, however, in that relatively few players, especially in the UK, go through further and higher education before embarking on their professional careers. In American sports, it's the norm for players to emerge from the generous scholarships of the collegiate system and take to the professional ranks, degree in hand; whereas in Britain, plenty of athletes, rowers and rugby union players hold degrees, largely because it's often at university where they hone their skills and begin to compete at a high level. In football, though, possessing a degree is pretty much the exception to the rule, primarily because those players who are of the requisite standard to make it in the game are usually discovered by clubs at a very young age, and while education is still an important part of their development, it often takes a back seat to the bigger goal of becoming a professional player.

That's not to say that there haven't been any graduates in football. In fact, there are plenty. Former Leeds United and Sheffield Wednesday central defender David Wetherall combined playing for Leeds with his course at the University of Sheffield, eventually earning a first-class degree in Chemistry. Iain Dowie has a degree in Engineering from the University of Hertfordshire and Steve Coppell completed a degree in Economics and Economic History from the University of Liverpool while playing for Tranmere Rovers. Then there was the late Brazilian star, 'Doctor' Socrates, who played for Botafogo in Brazil while simultaneously studying for a degree in Medicine at his local university Faculdade de Medicina de Ribeirão Preto; and today, of course, there's Juan Mata, Chelsea's Spanish star, who is currently studying for not one, but two degrees (Marketing and Sports Science) at Madrid's Universidad Camilo José Cela.

Frank Lampard registered an IQ in excess of 150... and placed him close to the IQs of Albert Einstein and Microsoft founder Bill Gates.

But such footballers with a proven track record in higher education are rare. Indeed, even those who read a broadsheet newspaper are still regarded with suspicion, as Chelsea and England's Graeme Le Saux discovered during his playing career. With a middle-class upbringing in the Channel Islands and a couple of A-levels to his name, the England left-back was often cast in the role of a football intellectual but also found himself the victim of baseless rumours purely because of his background and education.

If anything, it pays to keep your intellect to yourself in professional football, even if it is something you should be proud of. Until recently, for example, the Chelsea and England midfielder Frank Lampard had slipped under the radar as one of football's more intellectually-gifted players but in 2009, the doctor at Chelsea Football Club, Bryan English, conducted IQ tests with all of the playing staff at Stamford Bridge and discovered that Lampard registered an IQ in excess of 150. Indeed, his score, according to English, was one of the highest ever recorded in the test and placed him close to the IQs of Albert Einstein and Microsoft founder Bill Gates (both measured at 160) and far ahead of the former US President Bill Clinton who has a reported score of 137. It would also place him in the most intelligent 0.1 per cent of the population and his exploits soon earned him the nickname of 'The Professor' in the Chelsea dressing room as well.

But Lampard is unusual among the UK's professional players, not simply because he has a remarkably high IQ but also because he was educated at a fee-paying establishment: Brentwood School in Essex. It was an opportunity that helped him gain 12 GCSEs including a Grade A in Latin. And yet an increasing number of

More than a third of Team GB's medal winners came from public schools, despite only 7 per cent of the school population attending those establishments.

British sports stars are now emerging from the nation's public school system. At the London 2012 Olympics, for example, more than a third of Team GB's medal winners came from public schools, despite only 7 per cent of the school population attending those establishments. This disparity, however, was more marked in some sports than others. In rowing, more than half the gold medallists were privately educated, with less than a third emerging from the state system. In boxing, meanwhile, all the medallists were state-educated while all but one of the 12 medal-wining cyclists also came from state comprehensives.

Of course, this is largely down to the fact that many of the sports at which Team GB excelled were those not routinely taught at state schools, primarily because they have neither the facilities nor the funds to make them available to their students. But it's an advantage that also holds true across the broader academic progress of privately educated students. In A-level results, for example, private school pupils are four times more likely to achieve the top grades than comprehensive pupils. Indeed, an analysis of A-level results in 2009 revealed that 32.6 per cent of privately schooled A-level candidates gained three A grades, compared to just 8.1 per cent in comprehensive schools.[2]

While Lampard's IQ is unusual in football circles, it's not so remarkable in the wider world of sport, where there's a long list of stars who not only have an IQ to match the midfielder but also boast membership of MENSA, the organization for super-intelligent people. To become a member of MENSA, you must score at or above the 98th percentile on any one of a number of approved intelligence tests, and there are plenty of sports stars who have done just that including the British Olympic gold medallist swimmer Adrian Moorhouse, boxer Nicky Piper and Finland's double World Rally champion, Marcus Grönholm. Meanwhile, former WBA Cruiserweight champion Bobby Czyz was so proud of his membership of MENSA that he even took to the ring against Evander Holyfield in 1996 wearing a MENSA T-shirt.

While the beauty of sport is that most participants can compete against one another without referral to their academic prowess or otherwise, there is one sport that still requires would-be players to sit an exam before they sign up. In the US, all college players hoping to be drafted into the National Football League (NFL) are required to sit the Wonderlic Cognitive Ability Test before they can play. The Wonderlic is a 12-minute exam in which entrants have to answer as many of the 50 multiple choice questions as they can, and it's commonly used by American employers to test a new recruit's suitability for a job.[3]

In the Wonderlic, a score of 20 indicates average intelligence and equates to an IQ of around 100. In the years that the NFL players have been taking it, they have recorded an average of 21 – which, for the record, is the same average score as general clerical workers achieve. Of course, there's a huge range of scores that have been posted by NFL players, from Pat McInally, the Harvard student and Cincinnati Bengals wide receiver who scored a perfect 50 (the only player in history to do so), to Junior Rosegreen of Auburn University, who made the lowest-ever score in 2004 – just 2, some 13 points lower than the average score of a warehouse worker.[4]

For the record, Rosegreen never did make it into the NFL.

THE CLEVEREST POSITIONS IN THE NFL

According to the Wonderlic Test, even smart guys are crazy enough to play grid iron.

Offensive tacklers 26	Middle Linebackers 19
Centres 25	Cornerbacks 18
Quarterbacks 24	Wide Receivers 17
Guards 23	Fullbacks 17
Tight Ends 22	Halfbacks 16
Safeties 19	

... AND HOW THEY COMPARE TO OTHER PROFESSIONS

According to Wonderlic, an NFL offensive tackler's intelligence is comparable to a newswriter.

Chemist 31	Bank Teller 22
Programmer 29	Clerical Worker 21
Newswriter 26	Security Guard 17
Sales 24	Warehouse 15

Source: *The New Thinking Man's Guide to Pro Football* by Paul Zimmerman.

NOTES & SOURCES
1. *'Dealing With It'*, Guardian, *Weekend section, May 15, 1999.*
2. *'Gap Between Private and State Schools Grows'*, Daily Telegraph, *February 20, 2010.*
3. *'Taking Your Wonderlics'*, *Jeff Merron, espn.go.com.*
4. The New Thinking Man's Guide to Pro Football, *Paul Zimmerman, Simon & Schuster, 1984*

20. YOU ARE WHAT YOU TWEET
Do sporting superstars really care about other people?

While social networks have fundamentally changed the way that we communicate in the early twenty-first century, they have also presented high-profile celebrities – and in particular, sportsmen and sportswomen – with an ideal opportunity to 'connect' with their fan base, or mount what more cynical observers might describe as a 'brand extension' exercise aimed at placating sponsors and agents.

Yes, at the mere click of a mouse the modern-day sports star can tell the world about the key events in his or her life and career or, as is more often the case, the extremely trivial things that, on the face of it, would appear to be of little interest to anyone. Whether it's Manchester United's Wayne Rooney tweeting pictures of his new hair transplant, NBA star Delonte West asking where he can get his favourite snack abroad ("Donde esta la Krispy Kreme in Barcelona Yo?") or snooker's Mark Allen offering his views on China ("This place is horrendous! Dead cat found this morning. Any wonder this place stinks! Must be dead cats all round the town!!"), it can be immediate and often insignificant. It could be Arsenal footballer Jack Wilshere breaking some truly seismic news during his recuperation from injury ("I have just moved from the sofa to my bed!!"), Spurs striker Darren Bent urging the Tottenham chairman Daniel Levy to finalise his transfer ("Do I wanna go Hull City NO. Do I wanna go stoke NO do I wanna go sunderland YES so stop f****** around, Levy. Sunderland are not the problem in the slightest."), or San Diego Chargers cornerback Antonio Cromartie complaining about team catering ("Man we have 2 have the most nasty food of any team. Damn can we upgrade 4 str8 years the same ish [sic] maybe that's y we can't we [sic] the SB [Super Bowl] we need."). Yes, the Twittersphere is now the forum for most vital breaking sports news.

It's also become a global arena for a fiercely contested battle for fans, a place where the popularity of sports stars and shameless self-publicists is judged not by the size of their salaries but the number of followers they have. Indeed, the most popular of stars from the world of sport can now boast Twitter followings running into the tens of millions. At time of writing, Real Madrid striker Cristiano Ronaldo, for example, has almost 12.5 million followers – for the record over a million more people than populate his native Portugal. His team-mate, the Brazilian midfielder Kaka, is only a couple of hundred thousand followers behind, with a following so large that you would need over 143 Bernabéu Stadiums to accommodate them, should they all decide to come and watch him play.

The evidence suggests that while sports stars have the time to tweet, they simply don't have the time to truly engage, or 'connect', with the rest of the online community.

While they clearly enjoy having their egos stroked, brands bolstered and careers validated (albeit virtually), interest in all things online doesn't appear to extend to taking any real interest in other people's lives. An examination of the ratio of the number of followers each person has, as opposed to the number of people they are following, reveals that for the most part, the sporting top brass really couldn't care less what others are doing. At the time of writing, for every 247,052 people who follow Ronaldo, for example, he follows just one other person. But he's not the worst offender. Former Brazilian international Ronaldinho follows just 10 of the 175 million registered users on Twitter, despite having close to 4.5 million followers himself.

Perhaps they are extremely selective about who or what they follow, or maybe they're more concerned with amassing as many followers as possible, but the evidence suggests that while sports stars have the time to tweet, they simply don't have the time to truly engage, or 'connect', with the rest of the online community. But is that just the norm when it comes to high-profile Twitter users? The number one-ranked person on Twitter, for instance, is the pop singer Lady Gaga (@ladygaga), who has 28,413,906 followers and who follows some 137,956 other people, giving her a ratio of 206. Just behind her comes the teenage heartthrob Justin Bieber (@justinbieber), who as well as being extremely active on Twitter – he has posted nearly 17,800 tweets compared to Gaga's 1,718 – has 26,654,256 followers and follows 123,089 (a ratio of 217). One notch down at number three, though and the results are not so impressive.

Californian singer Katy Perry (@katyperry) may boast some 25,085,809 followers on Twitter but she follows just 108 people, giving her a ratio of 232,276 – a figure more in keeping with those in the higher echelons of the sports Twittersphere. However, they could all learn a lesson from sixth-placed Tweeter on the Top 100 list: US President, Barack Obama (@BarackObama). He may have 18,573,825 followers – around 1 million less than Britney Spears (@britneyspears) – but he also follows 674,240 people, giving him a ratio of just 28. And while he may have a team tweeting on his behalf, Obama still steps up to the plate every now and then, signing personal tweets with the slightly unappealing tag of 'BO'.

But it's not the only surprising trend from the list. With eight of the top-10 sports tweeters emanating from the world of football, it's clear that the soccer constituency is one of the most active (and therefore valuable) online communities, although the three players propping up the list, the Barcelona FC trio of Andres Iniesta, Cesc Fabregas and Gerard Pique, are not exactly the sort of athletes one might expect to figure so prominently in the table. That said, the presence of three Barcelona FC players in the top 10 shows just how popular the Catalan club has become in recent years, not least because these are also players who have gone on to win major international tournaments with Spain as well. What's intriguing, however, is that Barca's star turn

SPORTS TWEETERS...

Comparing their follower/following ratio, do Twitter's sports stars really care about your 140 characters?

Cristiano Ronaldo @Cristiano

Followers: **12,352,607**

Following: **50**

Followers to following ratio:

247,052

to

Kaka @KAKA

Followers: **12,256,127**

Following: **407**

Followers to following ratio:

30,113

to

Shaquille O'Neal @SHAQ

Followers: **6,109,751**

Following: **727**

Followers to following ratio:

8,404

to

LeBron James @KingJames

Followers: **5,807,598**

Following: **300**

Followers to following ratio:

19,359

to

Neymar Junior @Njr92

Followers: **5,044,223**

Following: **637**

Followers to following ratio:

7,919

to

Wayne Rooney @WayneRooney

Followers: **4,733,516**

Following: **120**

Followers to following ratio:

39,446

to

Ronaldinho Gaucho @10Ronaldinho

Followers: **4,408,608**

Following: **10**

Followers to following ratio:

440,861

to

Andres Iniesta @andresiniesta8

Followers: **4,163,897**

Following: **34**

Followers to following ratio:

122,468

to

Cesc Fabregas @cesc4official

Followers: **3,928,812**

Following: **100**

Followers to following ratio:

39,228

to

Gerard Pique @3gerardpique

Followers: **3,776,156**

Following: **260**

Followers to following ratio:

14,524

to

... AND HOW THEY COMPARE TO CELEBRITY TWEETERS

Lady Gaga @ladygaga

Followers: **30,403,069**

Following: **137,345**

Followers to following ratio:

221

to

Justin Bieber @justinbieber

Followers: **29,095,290**

Following: **122,684**

Followers to following ratio:

237

to

Britney Spears @britneyspears

Followers: **21,167,116**

Following: **412,742**

Followers to following ratio:

51

to

Barack Obama @BarackObama

Followers: **21,000,959**

Following: **671,660**

Followers to following ratio:

31

to

Ellen DeGeneres @TheEllenShow

Followers: **14,059,235**

Following: **47,147**

Followers to following ratio:

298

to

Source: Twitter.com, August 13, 2012

and the man generally acknowledged to be the world's greatest football player, Argentinian Lionel Messi, does not eclipse them all. That, primarily, is because there are at least three Twitter sites claiming to be the 'official' pages of Lionel Messi, a fact which, on the face of it, suggests the Argentine doesn't go anyway near Twitter in the first place.

NOTES & SOURCES
1. *Twitter.com, August 13, 2012.*

21. IS PARTICIPATION SPORT DESTINED TO DIE?
Will future generations just watch rather than play sport?

In the 2008 Pixar Animation Studios film *WALL·E*, the inhabitants of Earth have left a heavily-polluted planet behind them, taking to the skies in luxury spaceships where their every whim can be catered for from the comfort of high-tech chairs and where touch-screen table service from high-speed robots means they never have to even get up. Corpulent, inactive and entirely reliant on technology, they grow ever fatter, incapable of doing almost anything for themselves.

It may be a funny glimpse into another world but it's one that may not be so far from the truth. In modern-day Britain, you see, children are getting fatter and it's a worrying trend, not least because they are twice as likely to get fat as their counterparts across the English Channel in France. According to the latest figures from the National Child Measurement Programme, around a third of all children in England will be overweight or obese by the tie they leave primary school.[1]

In fact, there are myriad reasons suggested why Britain's children are increasingly overweight. Busier roads, low income, poor diet, 'stranger danger', computer games consoles – the reasons for the creeping inactivity of the children of the United Kingdom have been attributed to many things. But what part does sport, and the lack of taking part, play in the increasing indolence of the UK's younger generation?

There is no doubt that the benefits of playing sport go far beyond improving just one's physical fitness. For children, it can be the perfect vehicle for teaching everything from self-discipline to decision-making, from fostering team spirit to learning how to lose graciously. It's even good for the side of their education with nearly 44 per cent of teachers regarding sportier children as being better behaved and more able to concentrate in class than those who adopt a more sedentary lifestyle.[2]

The trouble, however, is convincing them to play it in the first place. A poll for British Triathlon and Tata Steel in March 2011 revealed that of the 1,500 children (aged 6–15) questioned, 10 per cent could not ride a bike, 15 per cent were unable to swim and some 22 per cent had never run a distance of 400 metres or more. Fifteen per cent meanwhile admitted they had never played any kind of sport with their parents. What was particularly worrying, however, was the reliance the poll found on gadgets and technology.

One-third of the children questioned said they did not own a bike while more than three-quarters (77 per cent) said they had a games console and 68 per cent said they owned a mobile phone of their own.

One-third of the children questioned said they did not own a bike while more than three-quarters (77 per cent) said they had a games console and 68 per cent said they owned a mobile phone of their own. Moreover, in the week before the poll was conducted, just 46 per cent of the children had ridden their bikes and 34 per cent had swam a length of the pool. Seventy three per cent, however, had played a video game.[3]

With that in mind, it's worth examining other nations to see how their children play sport and, crucially, why they do it. In Australia, a nation with a rich sporting heritage and a climate that's conducive to outdoor activities, 63 per cent of children aged 5–14 years take part in at least one sport (outside of the PE they have at school) with boys (70 per cent) keener to do it than the girls (56 per cent).[4]

But if that figure sounds impressive, it's nothing compared to Scotland. Often criticised for its national diet and rates of heart disease, it was a survey by the Scottish Government in 2008 that revealed some astonishing results, with 96 per cent of secondary school students taking part in at least one sporting activity outside of school PE lessons and not organised by school. What is key here is that these were not after school clubs, these were children actively seeking out physical activity.[5]

Although it's tempting to assume that children only take up a particular sport because of parental or perhaps peer pressure, two studies in the United States have found something altogether more startling. In 1990, Dr Martha Ewing and Dr Vern Seefeldt of the Youth Sport Institute at Michigan State University polled 10,000 boys and girls (aged 10–18) from 11 major cities in nine US states, requesting them to complete a questionnaire asking for the reasons they participated in sport outside of the compulsory sport they played at school. The top answer for both boys and girls was 'fun'. Winning, meanwhile, was only tenth on the boys list of responses and 13th on that of the girls, suggesting that pleasure rather than any obsession with performance was the key motivator in persuading children to play sport.

More recently, Ewing and Seefeldt's findings have been reinforced in a study by Peter Barston, a sophomore student at Fairfield College Preparatory School, Connecticut, who had been one of Ewing and Seefeldt's original subjects and who had decided to conduct his own local version of their study. He created a single-page form for respondents to fill in with just 11 reasons for why a student might choose to play sport. Having sampled 725 students across the junior football and basketball leagues in Darien County, he found that the overwhelming reason they played was for nothing other than sheer enjoyment. No dreams of the big time or of starring in the Super Bowl, no long-term plan to win a college scholarship... just fun. In fact, 'fun' was the highest response from boys and girls in every grade from fourth to eighth, with almost twice as many children in basketball (95 per cent of boys and 98 per cent of girls) maintaining that it was more important than winning.[6]

It's data like this that scotches the idea that kids only tend to play competitive sport if they happen to be good at it or because there is some kind of parental pressure to do so, but in the US at least, it's part of a trend that has actually seen falling levels of inactivity among children aged 6–12. The Physical Activity Council's (PAC) comprehensive annual report into sports, fitness and recreation participation in the USA – the 2012 Participation Report – found that inactivity rates fell in this age group from 16.6 per cent in 2010 to 16 per cent in 2011, while the rates in the 13–17 age group also fell from 16.7 per cent to 16.4 per cent. What these changes illustrate is that if a country with a poor health record like the USA can begin to make inroads into its problems with obesity and all-round inactivity, then it can't be an impossible task for other developed nations too.

Those adults who had three or more PE lessons each week between the ages of 13 and 17 were far more likely to engage in team sports and outdoor activities when they had grown up.

The key, of course, is what drives children and, indeed, adults to commit to playing sport. Intriguingly, one of the most interesting findings of the 2012 PAC report was that those children aged 6–11 who were exposed to physical education regularly at school were more likely to be active and interested in sport when they became adults.

Similarly, those adults who had three or more PE lessons each week between the ages of 13 and 17 were far more likely to engage in team sports and outdoor activities when they had grown up.[7]

All of which demonstrates just how important school sport is not just for individual children but for the long-term health of the nation. But is the UK really that bad in terms of its child participation in sport? Well, yes and no. On one hand obesity levels among children in England are rising with 33.4 per cent of Year 6 pupils (age 10–11), for example, classed as overweight or obese[8]; but on the other, there are large numbers of children seemingly bucking the trend towards more sedentary lifestyles. The Taking Part Survey of 2010–11 found that 85 per cent of 5–10 year-olds had participated in sports activities outside of school time in the four weeks prior to the survey while 95 per cent of 11–15 year-olds had done the same.

The key, it seems, is what your parents do. Not standing on the touchline screaming instructions, or sending you out for another tennis session at the crack of dawn, but what they actually do in terms of physical activity. The Health Survey for England 2008 found that more boys aged 2–10 met the recommendations for physical activity each week if their parents also met theirs, while those boys aged 11–15 achieved their targets, but only if their fathers did. Similarly, among both of these age groups, more boys were in the low activity category if their parents were also in this group. Among the girls, however, the activity levels of the parents made comparatively little difference.

And therein lies the problem. While boys seems generally more predisposed to taking part in sport, all the evidence suggests that girls, across the board, are much more likely to opt out of PE and any extra-curricular sport, with levels of activity beginning to tail off at secondary school; and while there is little difference in the amount of time 12 year-old boys and girls spend in their PE classes, when the girls hit 14 they spend as much as 44 minutes less a week doing PE than boys of the same age and nearly 70 minutes less at age 15.[9]

NOTES & SOURCES

1. *www.dailymail.co.uk/news/article-2257518/Make-high-levels-fat-sugar-salt-childrens-food-ILLEGAL-say-Labour.*
2. *BT 'Coaching For Life' survey, December 2011.*
3. *www.bbc.co.uk/news/education-13278317.*
4. *Children's Participation in Culture and Leisure Activities (CPCLA) Survey, 2009.*
5. *Children's Participation in Culture and Sport Survey, 2008.*
6. *www.sportsreasons.com.*
7. *2012 Participation Report, The Physical Activity Council's (PAC) annual report into sports, fitness and recreation participation in the US.*
8. *NHS National Child Measurement Programme, School Year 2010/11.*
9. *Children's Participation in Culture and Sport Survey, 2008.*

22. THE SHIRT ON YOUR BACK
A multi-billion industry – why football shirts are a serious bit of kit...

For many football fans, the wearing of your team's shirt is a matter of immense personal pride, irrespective of the colour scheme or the design that's been used. Yes, slipping on your club's replica kit is a clear and concise mission statement, a public pronouncement that pins your colours to the mast and identifies you to the world as a proud and loyal follower of a particular football club.

In the United Kingdom alone, the replica football shirt market is worth more than £300 million ($480 million), and it is by far the biggest market in Europe.[1] It's fair to say that it is a huge business in its own right. Where once a club would release a new shirt every two or three years, now every club has at least one new kit each season while some, such as Tottenham Hotspur, have launched three new kits – a home, an away and a third kit – every season for the past six years. For the fans, this represents a significant outlay if they want to wear the latest shirt but as far as the marketers go, it represents an irresistible opportunity because here, after all, is the chance to turn football fans into walking, talking sporting sandwich boards.

And it's big money. If you happen to be one of the major Premier League clubs, with a packed stadium every week, a burgeoning global fan base and an impressive trophy cabinet to match, you can demand the kind of cash that would keep a League Two club afloat for an entire season, maybe two. What's more, the sponsors will pay it. For the clubs, it's a no-brainer: they have a shirt that's seen on the television screen each and every week of the season, at home and abroad, and there's a big space in the middle of it doing nothing. Sponsors, meanwhile, wish to reach as many people as possible in as quick and relatively cost effective a way as they can. In short, it's a win-win situation.

Shirt sponsorship, in English football at least, is a comparatively recent innovation. While Liverpool were the first professional club in Britain to have a shirt sponsor when they joined forces with the Japanese electronics giant Hitachi in 1979, the first team to actually carry one was the Southern League's Kettering Town, who took to the field against Bath City on January 24, 1976 with the name of a local company, 'Kettering Tyres', emblazoned across their shirts. Kettering's groundbreaking new initiative was short-lived, though. Within days the Football Association had ordered the club to remove the branding as it contravened the FA's rules on sponsorship. Not to be outdone, Kettering simply changed the slogan to "Kettering T", arguing that it had nothing to do with the tyre company in question. Still the FA didn't approve, though, and faced with a then hefty £1,000 ($1,610) fine from the governing body, the Northamptonshire side was eventually forced to back down.

Revenues from shirt sponsorship deals across Europe's top leagues in England, Spain, Italy, Germany, France and the Netherlands of 2012 breached the £404 million ($650 million) mark for the first time.

Back in the 1970s, Kettering's ground-breaking shirt sponsorship deal provided them with a significant "four-figure sum"[2,] but fast forward a little over 35 years and the shirt deal is now as much part of the modern game as cup runs and corner flags. A recent survey by Sport+Markt revealed that the revenues from shirt sponsorship deals across Europe's top leagues in England, Spain, Italy, Germany, France and the Netherlands of 2012 breached the £404 million ($650 million) mark for the first time – proof, if it were needed, that it's another part of the game, like players' wages, that seems to fly in the face of the global economic downturn. Leading the way is the

English Premier League, whose clubs took in £120 million ($193 million) in shirt sponsorship in 2012–13, followed by Germany's Bundesliga with £97 million ($156 million), Italy's Serie A (£67 million), Spain's La Liga (£63.5 million), France's Ligue 1 (£42.2 million) and the Dutch Eredivisie (£32.1 million).[3]

Such are the sums on offer today that even those clubs who have staunchly resisted the idea of a sponsor's name being emblazoned across their shirts have been forced to rethink their strategy. Barcelona had long rejected the lure of shirt sponsorship, choosing instead to actually pay UNICEF for the privilege of carrying the children's charity's logo on their team shirts. But when times got tough at the Camp Nou, the offer of a record-breaking shirt deal from the Middle East proved too much to ignore. Having posted a loss of £64.36 million ($103 million) in the 2009/10 season, Barcelona was now saddled with a cumulative debt of £369.5 million ($594.8 million) so when the Qatar Foundation, a non-profit making organisation concerned with education projects, offered them a five-year shirt sponsorship deal worth £125 million ($200 million), it saw the UNICEF logo relegated to the back of the shirt and the branding of the new sponsor now adorned the front.

Leading the way is the English Premier League, whose clubs took in £120 million ($193 million) in shirt sponsorship in 2012–13, followed by Germany's Bundesliga with £97 million ($156 million), Italy's Serie A (£67 million) and Spain's La Liga (£63.5 million)...

Barca's maiden shirt deal eclipsed any other in the modern game, including those of their perennial rivals Real Madrid, who receive £20 million a year ($32 million) from the online betting company bwin, and Germany's Bayern Munich, who enjoy a £23 million-a-year ($36.8 million) deal with Deutsche Telekom.[4]

More recently, the issue of just who sponsors the clubs has been brought into focus by some of the deals that have been done. When Liverpool struck their four-year, £80 million

($129 million) arrangement with the international bank Standard Chartered in 2009, they couldn't have known that three years later the bank would be embroiled in a multi-billion dollar money-laundering scandal. Similarly, Newcastle United found themselves under scrutiny in the autumn of 2012 for signing a deal with Wonga.com, a short-term 'pay-day loan' company who typically charge interest of over 4,000 per cent per annum on their advances. In a clever piece of public relations, however, Wonga insisted that as part of their new sponsorship the name of Newcastle's Sports Direct stadium would revert to its traditional name, St James' Park – a move that seemed to appease most of the club's supporters.

In these austere times, however, it is difficult (and often impossible) for clubs to turn down sizeable offers of financial support from potential backers, especially as their expenditure on players' wages is so stratospherically high. So while the current Premier League champions, Manchester City, may enjoy the third-highest shirt sponsorship deal in Europe courtesy of a £20 million-a-season ($32 million) arrangement with Etihad Airways, the fact that their annual wage bill is £201 million ($323 million) should offer some idea about how clubs have to take the money while they can. Of course, Manchester City's case is a one-off in the UK. While they have a huge wage bill – it's almost as much as their annual turnover of £231 million ($372 million) – they also have owners, the Abu Dhabi United Group Investment and Development Limited, with extremely deep pockets.[5]

While it's clear what's in it for the clubs, what do the sponsors get from their collaboration? Well, put simply, the English Premier League is a communication tool unlike any other. In 2011, Sport+Markt estimated that the total global following of the English Premier League was 1.46 billion people, or around 70 per cent of the estimated 2.08 billion football fans in the world. Of those, some 615 million are supporters of one of the top flight's 20 clubs. But it's the television audience that's key here and in 2010/11, coverage of the Premier League reached 643 million homes around the world, up 11 per cent from 580 million in 2009/10. The net result of this increase was that the total cumulative in-home TV audience for the League rose from 2.9 billion to 3.9 billion, a figure that when added to the estimated 777 million viewers who watched away from their homes, gave the Premier League a total global audience of 4.7 billion people.

With a reach like this, it's hardly surprising that companies don't baulk at having to pay hundreds of millions to sponsor a club shirt. Indeed, Sport+Markt estimate that in 2010/11 the average Premier League club delivered £10 million ($16 million) of media value for their main shirt sponsor with 450,000 seconds of brand exposure. In other words, about 15,000 x 30-second TV adverts.[6]

Within nine months, though, the club had sold over 1 million shirts with 'Beckham' and '23' on the back and suddenly the transfer fee looked exceptionally good value.

The club shirt, then, has become an extremely valuable commodity and not simply because of the revenue it can garner for the teams, nor the benefits that the sponsors receive from the additional exposure. Increasingly, the shirt has also become a major factor in how clubs assess the value of a potential new recruit and for that matter, how they can offset any transfer fee. At the Spanish giants Real Madrid they have a tried-and-tested model of signing marquee players for astronomical sums, only to recoup a significant amount of the fee through sales of the shirt, with the new player's name and number on the back. When David Beckham signed for the club for £24.5 million ($39 million) in June 2003, for example, his arrival was greeted across the Spanish capital with the same kind of feverish delight usually reserved for visiting boy bands. Within nine months, the club had sold over 1 million shirts with 'Beckham' and '23' on the back and suddenly the transfer fee looked exceptionally good value.[7]

Similarly, eyebrows were raised in the summer of 2009 when Real Madrid smashed the transfer world record – less than a month after they had paid £56 million ($90 million) for the Brazilian Kaka – paying £80 million ($128 million) for Manchester United's Portuguese striker, Cristiano Ronaldo. Again, nine months later, the club announced that they had sold 1.2 million 'Ronaldo 9' team shirts in Madrid alone, with millions more being snapped up around the globe, the revenues from which exceeded £100 million ($160 million).[8]

It's a similar story in England, where arguably the country's greatest homegrown talent, the Manchester United striker Wayne Rooney, has led the way in terms of the number of shirts he has helped to sell with his name and number printed on

STAR PLAYER SHIRTS

The five top-selling player's names on replica shirts in the English Premier League.

WAYNE ROONEY
Team:
Manchester United

STEVEN GERRARD
Team:
Liverpool

FERNANDO TORRES
Team:
Chelsea

CRISTIANO RONALDO
Team:
Manchester United

FRANK LAMPARD
Team:
Chelsea

Source: www.premierleague.com, April 2012.

EUROPE'S TOP SHIRT SPONSORSHIP DEALS

Shirt sponsorship deals are part of modern football and generate significant revenue for clubs.

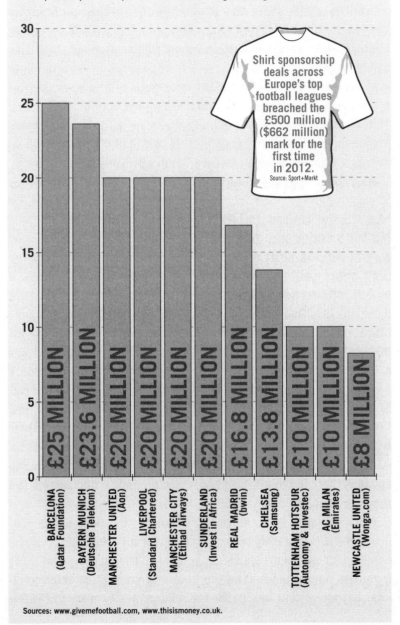

Shirt sponsorship deals across Europe's top football leagues breached the £500 million ($662 million) mark for the first time in 2012.
Source: Sport+Markt

BARCELONA (Qatar Foundation)	£25 MILLION
BAYERN MUNICH (Deutsche Telekom)	£23.6 MILLION
MANCHESTER UNITED (Aon)	£20 MILLION
LIVERPOOL (Standard Chartered)	£20 MILLION
MANCHESTER CITY (Etihad Airways)	£20 MILLION
SUNDERLAND (Invest in Africa)	£20 MILLION
REAL MADRID (bwin)	£16.8 MILLION
CHELSEA (Samsung)	£13.8 MILLION
TOTTENHAM HOTSPUR (Autonomy & Investec)	£10 MILLION
AC MILAN (Emirates)	£10 MILLION
NEWCASTLE UNITED (Wonga.com)	£8 MILLION

Sources: www.givemefootball.com, www.thisismoney.co.uk.

the back. A recent survey by Sporting ID, the company that makes the letters and numbers for the shirts, revealed that the England international was, in fact, the top-selling name used on replica shirts since the beginning of the English Premier League in 1992. The pull of Rooney, coupled with Manchester United's success on the field and their rich heritage in the game, has proved irresistible. Alongside Real Madrid, they continue to lead the way in replica shirt sales, both clubs selling an average of 1.4 million per season over the last five years, comfortably ahead of their nearest rivals. Reigning Premier League champions Manchester City, for instance, sell just 175,000 a season on average, placing them a distant 17th in a European sales list.[9]

And there are lots of kits to choose from. Where teams once used to have one home kit and one away kit, it's now common for professional teams to have a third change kit just in case there's a clash of colours that cannot be resolved. There's also the issue of the training kit too, which many clubs are now beginning to sell as a sponsorship option outside of the actual matchday strip deal. Manchester United, for example, is reported to receive another £10m ($16 million) for allowing the couriers DHL to sponsor their training wear. Tottenhan Hotspur, meanwhile, have received an additional £5 million ($8 million) a year for allowing Investec to sponsor their playing kit, but only in Cup games and not for the Premier League.

All of which leaves the truly committed fan with a financial headache if they really want a club kit for all occasions. But the expense doesn't end there. If you want the surname of your favourite player printed on the back of your replica shirt you'll have to pay for that too. In the UK, this typically costs £1 ($1.60)

Manchester United and Real Madrid continue to lead the way in replica shirt sales, both clubs selling an average of 1.4 million per season over the last five years, comfortably ahead of their nearest rivals.

THE WORLD'S BEST-SELLING FOOTBALL SHIRTS

In terms of units sold, the following football super powers lead the way in global replica shirt sales.

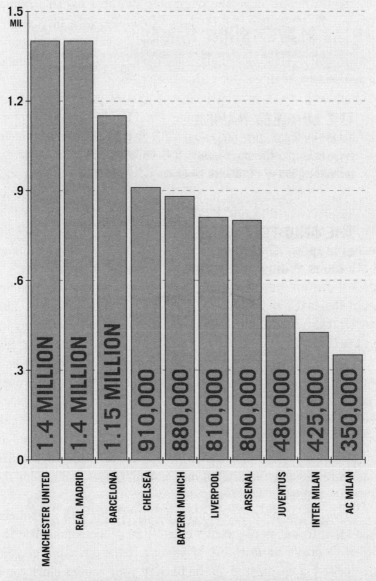

MANCHESTER UNITED	1.4 MILLION
REAL MADRID	1.4 MILLION
BARCELONA	1.15 MILLION
CHELSEA	910,000
BAYERN MUNICH	880,000
LIVERPOOL	810,000
ARSENAL	800,000
JUVENTUS	480,000
INTER MILAN	425,000
AC MILAN	350,000

Sources: Dr Peter Rohlmann / www.pr-marketing.de, www.sportingintelligence.com.
Notes: Average football shirt sales from 2007–08 to 2011–12.

per letter of a player's surname. So if your favourite player is Chelsea's Demba Ba you're in luck, but if it's Jan Vennegoor of Hesselink...

STAR PLAYER SHIRT NAMES

Essential to completing the look of any football replica kit and costing around £1 ($1.60) a letter, just what are the longest and shortest player names that you could have printed on the back of your shirt?

THE LONGEST NAMES
Roberto ABBONDANZIERI (Argentina) – **13 letters**
Jakub BLASZCZYKOWSKI (Poland) – **14 letters**
Jan VENNEGOOR OF HESSELINK (Holland) – **20 letters**

THE SHORTEST NAMES
Bo QU (China) – **2 letters**
Demba BA (Senegal) – **2 letters**

NOTES & SOURCES

1. *www.sports-insight.co.uk.*
2. *Derek Dougan, then Kettering manager and chief executive,* Guardian, *November 8, 2000.*
3. *European Football Kit Supplier Report 2012, Sport+Markt.*
4. *news.bbc.co.uk/sport1/hi/football/europe/9276343.stm.*
5. *'Premier League Club Accounts: How in Debt Are They?',* Guardian, *May 23, 2012.*
6. *'70% of the World's Football Fans Follow the Barclays Premier League',* *Sport+Markt, October 12, 2011.*
7. *'Real Money',* The Economist, *March 11, 2004.*
8. *'Cristiano Ronaldo shirt sales "have already paid off £80m ($128m) fee to Manchester United," Real Madrid claim,' Metro, April 15 2010.*
9. *www.sportingintelligence.com/2010/08/31/exclusive-manchester-united-lead-global-shirt-sales-list-liverpool-chase-as-england's-second-best-310805.*

23. INSULTS TO INJURIES
When sport gets its own back and why we all end up on the treatment table

When it comes to playing sport, deep down there is a part in men of a certain age that likes to believe they've still got 'it', whatever 'it' may be. It matters not that Father Time is getting the better of them, nor if the skills they believe they still possess in abundance were never really there in the first place; if there's a game to be played they will be there, trying to roll back the years.

And that, generally speaking, is a good thing. After all, the more exercise you can do, the less chance you have of suffering certain serious medical complaints in later life, such as coronary heart disease, diabetes, osteoporosis and hypertension. But while sport can be beneficial in all manner of ways, we tend to overestimate just how far we can push ourselves and the net result is that sooner or later, we are likely to pick up an injury. So while people may be circumnavigating the more serious complaints associated with inactivity and a sedentary lifestyle, the irony is that they are now suffering in other ways instead.

In England, there are 22 million sports injuries each year, or about 1.65 injuries per adult member of the population. It's a seemingly endless series of knocks, scrapes, bumps and bruises that can see each adult take an average of five days off work every year. For the most part, it's football that's doing the damage. Yes, the national game is responsible for 32 per cent of all sporting injuries in England, with rugby second (13 per cent) and running third (8 per cent).[1] Typically, the most common injury that adults sustain during these sports is muscle sprains and/or pulls, with cuts and bruises and tendon or ligament problems also registering highly.

The problem, it seems, is preparation or, as is more often the case, the lack of preparation. As children, of course, if you were ever asked to play football you would just slip on your boots and start playing at a moment's notice; but it's precisely this approach that gets adults of a certain age into trouble with failure, or even refusal, to warm up properly accounting for some serious soft tissue injuries. Indeed, 25 per cent of those who do suffer injury are forced to stop playing entirely, while 26 per cent refuse to seek treatment for their complaint. Predictably, men's personal pride also prevents them from admitting that any sporting injury they have sustained is actually their own fault, with 59 per cent blaming third-party involvement for their injury compared to just 22 per cent for women.[2]

It is basketball that yields the most injuries in the US, with 13.8 per cent of all sports injuries happening on the court.

Of course, it's a different picture in the USA, where other sports take precedence. While football, or soccer, is extremely popular, its playing base is focussed mainly among schoolchildren. Instead, it is basketball that yields the most injuries in the US, with 13.8 per cent of all sports injuries happening on the court. It's easy to see why. Here, after all, is an extremely explosive sport, played on a hardwood court, which not only places huge stress on the tendons and ligaments but can also see players laid low by barging or flying elbows. That said, it's American football that has the highest incidence of injuries per 100 participants, with 18.8 compared to the 7.6 per 100 basketball players.[3]

What is common across all territories and sports, however, is the reason for the majority of injuries, and while third-party contact and general clumsiness will always see injuries happen, the difference in players' athleticism and fitness levels always increases the likelihood of injury too. What tends to exacerbate the problem is the natural competitive instinct of men who, even though they may be 15 or 20 years older than the guys they are playing against, will do their utmost to keep pace, even if that means weeks on the treatment table after the game. But as humans age, the body becomes less able to perform the more explosive movements such as jumping, turning and sprinting that it could in its prime, and simultaneously becomes more prone to sustaining soft tissue damage. Achilles tendon ruptures, for example, are much more common in people in their 30s and 40s than in those in their 20s.[4] Conversely, the injuries that under-18s suffer while playing sport tend to be those that occur from overuse, that's to say they're playing too much sport[5] and whether

In the UK, for instance, there are around 10,000 injuries on golf courses that require hospital treatment, all of which are caused by errant shots from other golfers.

it's parental paranoia or genuine concern, nearly 40 per cent of children aged 5–14 who are injured in sport will seek medical assistance at hospital emergency departments.[6]

To avoid the typical sprains, tears and twists that afflict athletes of a certain age, it's perhaps advisable to take up a sport that offers a much greater chance of walking away without injury. Generally speaking, it is the non-contact sports, like golf, that are among the safest to play, although the repetitive motion of performing the swinging of a golf club can still place strain on the knees, hips and back. If anything, the real danger in golf comes from other players. In the UK, for instance, there are around 10,000 injuries on golf courses that require hospital treatment, all of which are caused by errant shots from other golfers.[7]

Racquet sports also offer some scope for safe sport. According to the National Center for Catastrophic Sport Injury Research in the US, tennis is, statistically, much safer than track and field or baseball. Over 25 years of research, the Center has found that there have been more than 500,000 track and field injuries across high schools in the States, while baseball registered some 400,000. Tennis, meanwhile, has less than 140,000 reports.

But any sport, no matter how innocuous in appearance, can lead to injury and just as hulking American football players crashing into each other seems destined to end in pain and problems, there are sports that although seemingly trouble-free, can still lead to injuries. Take darts, for example. During the course of a match a player can make as many as 3,700 steps to and from the board to retrieve his darts, which given that many of the players are not athletes in the strictest sense of the word can lead to fatigue. But it's the repetitive motion of releasing the dart that can cause serious issues. 'Darts-thrower's elbow', for example, is a medical condition now recognised in the *American Journal of Sports Medicine*, while 'Dartitis', the cramping condition that famously afflicted the five-times World Champion Eric Bristow, can also jeopardize a player's career.[8]

Similarly, the repetitive nature of snooker can also cause compound injuries in the back, shoulders and neck. There are

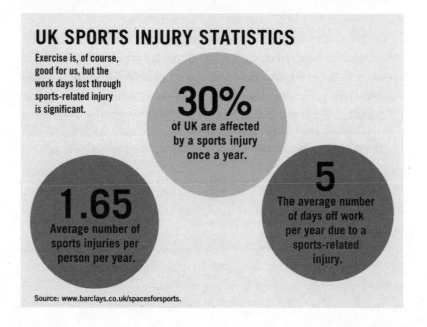

UK SPORTS INJURY STATISTICS

Exercise is, of course, good for us, but the work days lost through sports-related injury is significant.

30%
of UK are affected by a sports injury once a year.

1.65
Average number of sports injuries per person per year.

5
The average number of days off work per year due to a sports-related injury.

Source: www.barclays.co.uk/spacesforsports.

other dangers too, especially if you reach a high standard. In 2005, Steve Davis was forced to concede his match against Ricky Walden at the China Open when he began to feel unwell during the fourth frame. It was later revealed that he had run into a door frame while trying to escape a gang of eager autograph hunters.

WHEN SPORT IS HARMFUL!

This astonishing list of sports-related injury data was collected from US emergency room visits in 2006.

Number of Injuries	Sport and Common Injury Types
529,837	**Basketball** – Injured hands, sprained ankles, broken legs, eye and head injuries.
490,434	**Cycling** – Head injuries from falls, slipping while carrying bicycles, collisions with vehicles
460,210	**American Football** – Fractured wrists, chipped teeth, neck strains, head lacerations, dislocated hips and injured fingers.
275,123	**All-Terrain Vehicles and Minibikes** – Injuries resulting from riders being thrown from vehicles – Fractured wrists, hands and shoulder injuries, head cuts and abdominal strains.
274,867	**Baseball and Softball** – Head injuries from bats and balls. Ankle and hand injuries from running bases or sliding.
269,249	**General exercise and gym equipment** – Twisted and sprained ankles. Head injuries from falling backward from exercise balls.
186,544	**Football** – Twisted ankles and knees, and fractured arms.
164,607	**Swimming** – Head injuries from hitting the bottom of swimming pool, and leg strains
96,119	**Skiing and Snowboarding** – Head injuries. Various fractures, cuts to legs, arms and faces. Sprained knees or shoulders.
85,580	**Lacrosse, Rugby, & other Ball Games** – Head and facial cuts from getting hit by balls. Twisted and sprained ankles.

Source: US National Electronic Injury Surveillance System.

NOTES & SOURCES

1. *www.barclays.co.uk/spacesforsports.*
2. *Ibid*
3. *'A Comprehensive Study of Sports Injuries in the U.S.', American Sports Data, Inc., 2006.*
4. *'Most Hazardous Sports', Forbes.com, May 29, 2008.*
5. *www.sportssafety.org/sports-injury-facts.*
6. *Ibid.*
7. *www.golfcare.co.uk.*
8. *www.guardian.co.uk, July 26, 2008.*

24. SPORTING CLICHÉS DECONSTRUCTED
Uttered countless times by coaches, players and commentators, is there any truth to these overused expressions?

Sport, in all its many glorious guises, has a unique ability to inspire and enthrall. For the viewer or spectator, it can be surprising, uplifting and even, at times, life-affirming. For the participants who have strained every sinew in pursuit of glory though, it can be an experience that leaves them drained and it's understandable and entirely forgivable that in those moments after a match when a reporter suddenly thrusts a microphone into their faces, they find themselves unable to stop slipping into clichés. For those presenters and commentators sitting in the relative comfort of the studio without ever once breaking sweat, however, there really is no excuse.

"THEY'RE IN A LEAGUE OF THEIR OWN..."

This might be an oft-used line to suggest complete superiority, but nevertheless it remains an erroneous notion. By definition a league must contain sufficient teams or participants to fulfil a pre-arranged list of fixtures, so any team that does exist in a league of their own will not face any opponents and the competition cannot therefore be deemed a "league". The world's smallest league (affiliated to the Football Association) is in the Scilly Isles, where two teams, Garrison Gunners and the Woolpack Wanderers, play each other every Sunday over a 17-week season on the island of St Mary's. These two teams

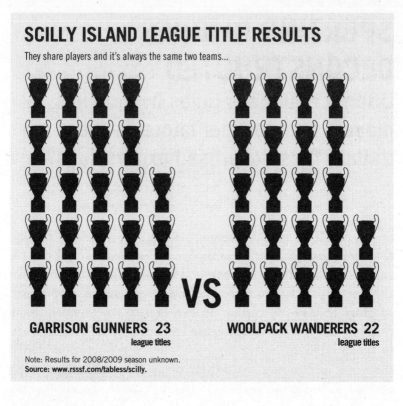

SCILLY ISLAND LEAGUE TITLE RESULTS

They share players and it's always the same two teams...

VS

GARRISON GUNNERS 23
league titles

WOOLPACK WANDERERS 22
league titles

Note: Results for 2008/2009 season unknown.
Source: www.rsssf.com/tabless/scilly.

also contest two Cup competitions: The Wholesalers Cup and the Foredeck Cup (played over two legs), and they begin each season with their now traditional curtain-raiser, the Charity Shield.[1]

"HE GAVE 110 PER CENT..."

A favourite of the post-match managerial press conference, the idea that someone can contribute more than is physically possible continues to fascinate the nation's coaches, irrespective of the health dangers associated with significant over-exertion. During exercise, the recommended target heart-rate zone is up to 85 per cent of the maximum heart rate. While training at 110 per cent of your maximum heart rate is likely to end in death, even exercising at 110 per cent of the recommended target heart rate – ie 93.5 per cent of the maximum heart rate – can also lead to significant medical problems, even if you are physically fit. A study by the *Canadian Medical Association Journal* in 2002[2] found that regularly exceeding the 85 per cent recommendation could lead to poorer heart-rate recovery levels, as well as potentially life-threatening ventricular tachycardia (or fast heart rhythms). Those with no history, or none of the risk factors of coronary heart disease, may be able to exceed the recommended heart rate without any

> **Regularly exceeding the 85 per cent recommendation could lead to poorer heart-rate recovery levels, as well as potentially life-threatening ventricular tachycardia.**

discernible ill effects, but it can expose athletes to a greater risk of musculoskeletal injury.

Moreover, it's been proven that exercising at levels in excess of your recommended maximum heart rate can have the opposite effect: increasing fatigue, decreasing performance and making the body weaker, not stronger. The problem, however, is that a coach declaring his striker "gave 85 per cent today" not only suggests indolence on the player's part but also sits badly with the fans, who rarely demand anything less than 110 per cent.

"THEY'RE TOO GOOD TO GO DOWN..."

Fact. No team in the history of the sport has ever been relegated despite being better than those who finished above them. It's quite simple – league tables, based on performances, do not lie. The only possible exception to this rule is those teams who can boast a better playing record but have points deducted for other reasons, such as fielding ineligible players or, as in the case of Arsenal and Manchester United in the 1990–91 First Division season, for on-field ill-discipline. Point deductions for a club going into administration can also mean that while having a better playing record, a team may still be relegated. In the 2004/05 Football League One campaign, for example, Wrexham won 53 points, a total that would have been sufficient for them to take 19th place in the final standings, but having had 10 points deducted for going into administration, the Welsh club found themselves with just 43 points and 22nd place in the final table – consigning them to League Two for the next season.[3]

One other notable example was the case of Juventus in the Italian Serie A of 2006. The Turin giants were relegated after becoming embroiled in a match-fixing scandal and this despite being a team littered with internationals such as Gianluigi Buffon, Pavel Nedved, Fabio Cannavaro, Zlatan Ibrahimovic and Alessandro Del Piero. All of which begs the question, why exactly did they need to fix the matches in the first place?

"THE KEEPER ROSE LIKE A SALMON ..."

While salmon are known for their ability to leap they are not the highest jumping fish of all. Thresher sharks, for example, have been known to jump much higher, sometimes up to 20 feet (6 metres) clear of the water. Indeed, the highest recorded jump made by a salmon was a vertical one of 12 ft (3.65 m) at the Orrin Falls in Ross-shire, Scotland. While the height that a salmon is capable of leaping depends on the relative depth of the water, it's safe to assume that if a goalkeeper were able to attain such a feat, he would clear the 8 ft (2.4 m) height of the crossbar, which in all likelihood would mean that the original shot was already going comfortably over the bar and didn't actually require a leap of such magnitude in the first instance. That said, if he could jump like a thresher shark, then he would probably be playing basketball.[4]

"THERE ARE NO EASY GAMES AT THIS LEVEL..."

A line often said by coaches and players so as not to disrespect upcoming opponents, there is significant evidence to suggest that across all sports there are certain fixtures, or 'easy games', where most teams can realistically expect to walk away with an extremely straightforward victory. In international cricket, for example, Bangladesh has won just three of their 75 Test matches[5] while in ice hockey Panama sit hopelessly at the bottom of the world rankings[6] and in football the San Marino international football team, already mentioned in this book, have won only one game from 118, scoring just 19 goals and conceding 485 goals[7]. Historically, there had also been occasions where opposition teams must have been looking forward to certain games

The Detroit Lions lost all 16 of their games (the first team in history to do so) while the Cleveland Spiders have gone down in history as the worst baseball team ever after a disastrous season in 1899 when they lost 134 games.

more than others. In 2008 in America's National Football League (NFL), for instance, the Detroit Lions lost all 16 of their games (the first team in history to do so), while the Cleveland Spiders have gone down in history as the worst baseball team ever after a disastrous season in 1899 when they lost 134 games, with 101 of those coming in away fixtures. In golf, meanwhile, the British, and then the Great Britain and Ireland Ryder Cup team, won just three out 25 Ryder Cup matches against a United States team who routinely embarrassed them between 1927 and 1983. Indeed, this tended to be less of a competition and more of a cull. So whether it's genuine respect for their opponents or a thinly-veiled attempt to mask the anticipation of an easy victory, it's clear that when managers say that "there are no easy games at this level", they are wrong.

NOTES & SOURCES

1. *www.worldssmallestleague.co.uk.*
2. *www.cmaj.ca.*
3. *www.football-league.co.uk.*
4. *www.atlanticsalmontrust.org.*
5. *www.stats.espncricinfo.com*
6. *www.fih.ch*
7. *www.fifa.com*

THE TRUE VALUE OF WINNING A TROPHY
Nothing beats holding up that famous trophy, but all that glitters is not gold

Though enthusiastic school teachers and eternally optimistic parents may often console their kids that sport is not about the winning but actually about the taking part, those who do it for a living – the players, athletes, coaches and managers – will say something quite different. Winning is everything and for the most part, the financial rewards or prize money on offer are not really what persuades individuals to put themselves on the line in the pursuit of glory. No, it's that magical and memorable moment, the culmination of the years of dedication and self-sacrifice, when a trophy is lifted above a player's head that makes all the pain and pressure worthwhile.

It's one of the quirks of sporting endeavour, however, that in one sport the teams may be playing for a trophy such as ice hockey's Stanley Cup, which is big and shiny and almost impossible to lift, while in another, like cricket's Ashes Test series between England and Australia, participants fight it out for a tiny terracotta urn. Here, the trophy is a token and merely a prized symbol of the victory achieved. In short, it matters not one jot what the monetary value happens to be: the real value lies in what it takes to win it. That said, some of the world's most famous trophies are worth significant sums of cash and in an austere age where precious metals (and even less precious metals) reach record prices, the winners would be well served to invest some of their prize money in a secure cabinet in which to house them all.

Here are some of the world's most famous trophies along with an indication of base metal values if, heaven forbid, they were ever melted down and sold for scrap:

THE TRUE VALUE OF SPORT'S GREATEST PRIZES

They are iconic symbols of sporting success, but what would they be worth if they were sold for scrap?

164.5CM

125CM

91.5CM **90CM**

74CM

61CM

150 CM

100

50

0

THE BORG-WARNER TROPHY
Awarded for: Winning the Indianapolis 500 automobile race.
Origins: Created in 1935 for £6,235 ($10,000) and first awarded in 1936.
Made from: Sterling silver
Weight: 49kg
Insurance value: £930,000 ($1.5 million)
Interesting fact: Winner of the 1950 Indianapolis 500, Johnnie Parsons, famously has his name misspelt on the trophy as 'Johnny' Parsons.

Physical scrap value: **£6,235 ($10,038)**

THE AMERICA'S CUP
Awarded for: Winning the America's Cup sailing race.
Origins: Created in 1848 by Britain's Garrard and Co and is the world's oldest active trophy.
Made from: Sterling silver
Weight: 15kg
Insurance value: £150,000 ($240,000)
Interesting fact: The trophy was first awarded in 1851 for a race around the Isle of Wight. The race was won by the schooner, *America* and the trophy renamed in its honour.

Physical scrap value: **£9,374 ($15,092)**

THE WOODLAWN VASE
Awarded for: The winner of the Preakness Stakes at Pimlico Race Course, Maryland.
Origins: Made by Tiffany and Co in 1860, it was first awarded in 1861.
Made from: Sterling silver
Weight: 11.33kg
Insurance value: £2.5 million ($4 million)
Interesting fact: , The trophy was hidden during the American Civil War to prevent soldiers from melting it down for use as ammunition.

Physical scrap value: **£7,080 ($11,398)**

THE STANLEY CUP
Awarded for: Winning the National Hockey League (NHL) playoffs.
Origins: First awarded in 1893 to an athletics club, first awarded as the NHL prize in 1927.
Made from: Silver-nickel alloy
Weight: 15.6kg
Insurance value: £930,000 (US$1.5 million)
Interesting fact: A new ring is added to the trophy base every 13 years to accommodate the names of the winners.

Physical scrap value: **£621 ($1,000)**

THE CHAMPIONS LEAGUE TROPHY
Awarded for: Winning the UEFA European Champions League.
Origins: The latest design dates from 1967, it was created by Swiss jeweler Jorg Stadelmann.
Made from: Sterling silver
Weight: 8.5kg
Interesting fact: Five-times winners of the Champions League or European Cup are allowed to keep the trophy. Once awarded in this way, a new trophy is commissioned.

Physical scrap value: **£4,753 ($1,677)**

THE COMMISSIONER'S TROPHY
Awarded for: Winning the Major League Baseball (MLB) World Series.
Origins: The trophy is regularly redesigned, the current trophy was created by Tiffany and Co in 1999.
Made from: Sterling silver
Weight: 14kg
Interesting fact: The trophy features 30 flags, representing each Major League Baseball team.

Physical scrap value: **£8,749 ($14,085)**

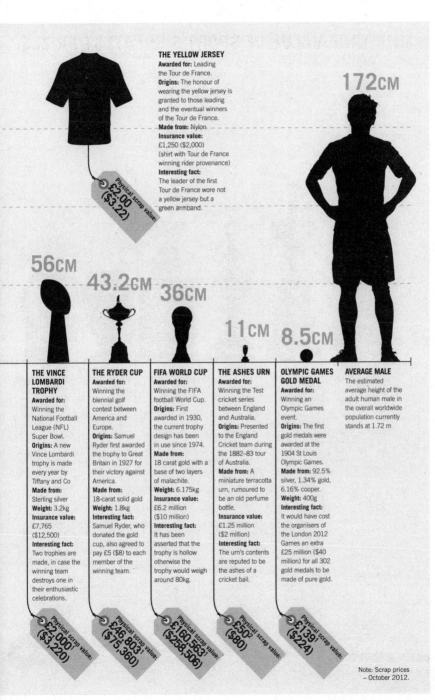

172CM

56CM

43.2CM

36CM

11CM

8.5CM

THE YELLOW JERSEY
Awarded for: Leading the Tour de France.
Origins: The honour of wearing the yellow jersey is granted to those leading and the eventual winners of the Tour de France.
Made from: Nylon
Insurance value: £1,250 ($2,000) (shirt with Tour de France winning rider provenance)
Interesting fact: The leader of the first Tour de France wore not a yellow jersey but a green armband.

Physical scrap value: £2.00 ($3.22)

THE VINCE LOMBARDI TROPHY
Awarded for: Winning the National Football League (NFL) Super Bowl.
Origins: A new Vince Lombardi trophy is made every year by Tiffany and Co
Made from: Sterling silver
Weight: 3.2kg
Insurance value: £7,765 ($12,500)
Interesting fact: Two trophies are made, in case the winning team destroys one in their enthusiastic celebrations.

Physical scrap value: £2,000 ($3,220)

THE RYDER CUP
Awarded for: Winning the biennial golf contest between America and Europe.
Origins: Samuel Ryder first awarded the trophy to Great Britain in 1927 for their victory against America.
Made from: 18-carat solid gold
Weight: 1.8kg
Interesting fact: Samuel Ryder, who donated the gold cup, also agreed to pay £5 ($8) to each member of the winning team.

Physical scrap value: £46,803 ($75,360)

FIFA WORLD CUP
Awarded for: Winning the FIFA football World Cup.
Origins: First awarded in 1930, the current trophy design has been in use since 1974.
Made from: 18 carat gold with a base of two layers of malachite.
Weight: 6.175kg
Insurance value: £6.2 million ($10 million)
Interesting fact: It has been asserted that the trophy is hollow otherwise the trophy would weigh around 80kg.

Physical scrap value: £160,563 ($258,506)

THE ASHES URN
Awarded for: Winning the Test cricket series between England and Australia.
Origins: Presented to the England Cricket team during the 1882–83 tour of Australia.
Made from: A miniature terracotta urn, rumoured to be an old perfume bottle.
Insurance value: £1.25 million ($2 million)
Interesting fact: The urn's contents are reputed to be the ashes of a cricket bail.

Physical scrap value: £50 ($80)

OLYMPIC GAMES GOLD MEDAL
Awarded for: Winning an Olympic Games event.
Origins: The first gold medals were awarded at the 1904 St Louis Olympic Games.
Made from: 92.5% silver, 1.34% gold, 6.16% cooper.
Weight: 400g
Interesting fact: It would have cost the organisers of the London 2012 Games an extra £25 million ($40 million) for all 302 gold medals to be made of pure gold.

Physical scrap value: £139 ($224)

AVERAGE MALE
The estimated average height of the adult human male in the overall worldwide population currently stands at 1.72 m

Note: Scrap prices – October 2012.

145

NOTES & SOURCES

1. *www.silverrecyclers.com.*
2. *www.ebay.com*

26. MUSIC TO AN ATHLETE'S EAR
Why an athlete's playlist can be the difference between winning and losing

It's an all too common sight these days: a football team's coach pulls up at an away ground and, as an expectant gaggle of autograph hunters awaits, off troop the players, each one with an expensive pair of oversized headphones pressed to his ears as he scurries into the stadium. And what about the London 2012 Olympic Games? If you observed any of the swimming or athletics events that took place there was always a handful of athletes arriving at the starting blocks with their earphones or headphones still in place, only ever removing them at the last minute before their race began.

But is there another reason for athletes' over-reliance on their MP3 players? The answer, unequivocally, is yes, and the iPod is fast becoming as vital a piece of training equipment as any other in the athlete's armoury. But research suggests that the benefits of listening to music go beyond mere mood enhancement or blocking out peripheral distractions. A recent joint study into the performance of elite triathletes by Peter Terry of the University of Southern Queensland, Toowoomba, and Costas Karageorghis of Brunel University, west London, revealed that synchronous music, wherein the length of an athlete's stride is matched to the tempo of the music, can have a metronomic effect on the body and increase an athlete's energy efficiency by 1–3 per cent and his endurance by up to 15 per cent. In short, the music, or rather the *right kind* of music, allowed them to run for longer.[1]

Terry and Karageorghis found that by using particular kinds of music that were selected based on scientific evidence rather than intuition, athletes could experience as much as a 10 per cent reduction in perceived exertion during a session of moderate intensity on a treadmill, and while that didn't apply to high-intensity workouts, it did help to make those tougher sessions more pleasurable. So while the efficacious effects of music can help to lower the perception of effort when athletes are training – that is to say it takes their mind off the pain their body is suffering – it can also be an extremely useful tool for increasing work capacity, and athletes tend to fill their playlists with those songs that give them the impetus and inspiration to push themselves that little bit harder.

There have been many scientific studies examining the effect that music can have on an athlete's training but broadly speaking, it is clear that listening to music while training can benefit everything from motivation and endurance levels to psychological wellbeing and actual performance. It is apparent, moreover, that synchronous music (where an athlete moves to the beat of the music) and asynchronous music (where he doesn't) are both effective in creating more productive training. Synchronous music, for example, is ideal in accompanying runs on the treadmill while asynchronous music can help to provide physiological distraction during a workout.

Crucially, the tempo of the songs that athletes choose should be roughly in accordance with the intended intensity of their training session.

Crucially, the tempo of the songs that athletes choose should be roughly in accordance with the intended intensity of their training session. So if an athlete is cycling at around 70 per cent of his aerobic capacity, mid-tempo music of around 115–125 beats per minute (bpm) will be more beneficial than faster music of 135bpm and over.

In his studies, Karageorghis also found that it is those songs those lyrics convey, suggest or encourage movement ('The Only Way Is Up' or 'Movin' On Up' and so on) and in which the lyrics concern overcoming adversity and achieving goals that produce the most significant results. It's a view reinforced by Britain's greatest-ever female marathon runner, Paula Radcliffe. "I put together a playlist and listen to it during the run-in," she said. "It helps psych me up and reminds me of times in the build-up when I've worked really hard, or felt good. With the right music, I do a much harder workout."

Karageorghis also found that using music in a team environment works equally well. To that end, he identified a team's preparation for a match as being split into three distinct phases: Visualisation, Pre-Match Motivation and Post-Match Motivation, and created a playlist of specific songs in a set order, with each one having a higher bpm than the previous one. In the Visualisation stage before the event, this could mean starting off with something stirring like 'Abide With Me' (42bpm) and work up to David Bowie's 'Heroes' (113bpm) and even the theme from BBC's *Grandstand* (132bpm).

In the immediate Pre-Match Motivation stage, meanwhile, the songs need to suggest and promote notions of teamwork, camaraderie and a shared vision so that the team can take to the field pumped up and ready for the battle ahead. From Queen's 'We Are The Champions' (64bpm) through to The Farm's 'Altogether Now' and on to the exultant horns of Dario G's 'Carnival de Paris' (137bpm), these are songs designed to get the blood pumping.

Finally it's essential that the team reconvenes after the game to wind down, and in the final stage, Post-Match Motivation, the tempo of the songs needs to start higher and slow down, track by track. Here, the likes of 'Albatross' by Fleetwood Mac (67bpm) and Seal's 'Kiss From A Rose' (44bpm) help the players to return to a more normal heartbeat.[2]

But it's not just the professionals who use music as a motivator. Across the world, amateur athletes have come to rely on their playlists as a way of getting them through the tougher times in training and the punishment they endure when they're actually participating. Never was this more evident than in 2007 when the New York Marathon organisers, acting on a wider directive from USA Track & Field, announced that they were banning the use of iPods and MP3 players during the race for "health and safety" reasons.

For many runners, the idea that they would have to tackle the 26.2 miles without their motivational music was an affront to human rights. On the day of the race, and despite the threat of disqualification hanging over them, many runners simply chose to secrete their MP3 players in their shirts or sports bras before whipping them out as the race got underway, while others openly flouted the request and wore their earphones without a care for the consequences. Later, the organisers admitted that, in reality, they actually had no way of enforcing the ban among the 40,000 participants.

THE SONGS THAT INSPIRE SPORTS STARS...

Listening to the right music can be key to sporting success.

MO FARAH (5,000m & 10,000m)
2Pac – *Keep Your Head Up*

LEBRON JAMES (basketball)
Radiohead – *Bodysnatchers*

PAULA RADCLIFFE – (marathon)
Kanye West – *Stronger*

PHILLIPS IDOWU (triple jump)
Michael Mcdonald – *What a Fool Believes*

CHRIS HOY (cycling)
Chemical brothers – *Escape Velocity*

MICHAEL PHELPS (swimming)
Lil' Wayne – *I'm Me*

BEN AINSLIE (sailing)
Phil Collins – *In the Air Tonight*

TOM DALEY (diving)
Heather Small – *Proud*

JESSICA ENNIS (heptathlon)
Kanye West – *Monster*

ZACH VLAHOS (rowing)
Miley cyrus – *Party in the USA*

Sources: *Telegraph*, www.ca.sports.yahoo.com.

NOTES & SOURCES

1. *'Effects of synchronous music on treadmill running among elite triathletes.'* Journal of Science and Medicine in Sport, *2012, Peter C. Terry, Costas I. Karageorghis, Alessandra Mecozzi Saha, and Shaun. D'Auria.*
2. www.*performance.fourfourtwo.com/health/psychology/music-to-improve-your-performance.*

27. WHAT IF WE ALL ATE LIKE SUMO WRESTLERS?

And the impact it would have on society and the global economy

Top-level sport is a career path that only a few fortunate people get to follow. For the most part, it's a lifestyle that requires dedication, devotion and no small amount of self-sacrifice for athletes to achieve success. Even apparently non-athletic sports such as darts and snooker require endless hours of practice and routine, even if they don't need a six-pack and some track shoes.

But discipline comes in many forms and it's not always about how many laps you've done, or how many bench presses you're capable of. For many athletes it means eschewing little luxuries, like a little drink and a late night. For others, it means months of monk-like solitude, enduring harsh training camps while detached from all life and reality. In the world of sumo wrestling, where Shinto ritual and tradition is everything, the *rikishi*'s dedication is never more evident than when it comes to their unique diet.

Yes, the training regime of the sumo wrestler is unlike any other athlete in modern sport. While they may appear to be morbidly overweight – and they certainly are – their condition is an artificial obesity, created by a strict diet designed to maximise bulk and increase physical presence when they enter the *dohyo*. And in a sport where weight gain is key and size really is everything, the lengths to which sumo wrestlers go to gain an advantage are simply extraordinary, putting their long-term health at serious risk and significantly reducing life expectancy.

But it's weight that is the key to their success in the sport and any *rikishi* who wants to reach the highest rank of *yokozuna* will need the bulk to back up their skills. The ideal fighting weight for a sumo wrestler is around 500 lb (226 kg) or 3.6 times the weight of an average human globally, or three times the weight of the average British adult.[1] There have been bigger *rikishi*, most notably Konishiki Yasokichi, whose 630 lb-frame (285 kg) earned him the nickname 'The Dump Truck', but typically, successful wrestlers usually weigh between 400 and 600 lb (181–272 kg). Now, given that the World Health Organisation recommends that a fully-grown adult male requires around 2,500 calories to maintain their weight, you may expect that sumo wrestlers, at roughly three times the size of a normal man, require three times the amount of calories; they don't. Typically, a sumo will consume around 20,000 calories a day, or to put it another way, the equivalent of 40.75 Big Mac burgers, each and every day.[2]

Yet theirs is not a grazing diet of steady, prolonged ingestion. Instead, sumo wrestlers will skip breakfast and then have two huge 10,000-calorie meals each day, punctuated by long, much-needed sleep. While it may seem as if sumo wrestlers can eat what they want and when they want, especially as the express intention is to gain weight, the sumo diet, like every aspect of their training, is actually extremely regimented. The staple dish of the dietary regime is *chankonabe*, a protein-rich stew with beef, fish, tofu and vegetables that they consume in huge quantities. It is not unusual for a *rikishi* to devour several large bowls and between five and 10 bowls of rice at one sitting. Unusually for an athlete in training, their diet can also include beer as it provides additional empty calories and a wrestler may have five or six pints during his lunch. Intriguingly, the *chankonabe* eaten during a tournament is only ever prepared using chicken, the idea being that as chickens walk on two legs, the sumo will also leave the *dohyo* on two legs – meaning, of course, that they have won.

In any other walk of life the consumption habits of a sumo wrestler might be considered vulgar and gluttonous, but in Japan the top-ranking *rikishi* are household names and fêted like film stars.

There are only 46 training stables and around 660 sumo wrestlers across all levels in Japan so while that may mean increased trade for the food stores in the locale of the actual stables the overall effect on the economy of Japan, where there are nearly 128 million people is virtually nil[3].

But if every person in Japan decided to eat like a sumo the effect would be truly seismic. Currently, Japan is the world's tenth biggest producer of rice, making some 10.6 million metric tonnes every year[4] while each Japanese person eats an average of 129 lb (58.5 kg) of rice per year[5]. Sumo wrestlers, meanwhile, eat a 2.2 lb (1 kg) of rice each and every day[6] while the average per capita intake of rice in the UK, by comparison, is just 10 lb (4.4 kg).[7]

If every person in Japan were to eat the same amount of rice as a sumo, ie 805 lb (365 kg) a year, Japan would need to produce over 66 million metric tonnes of rice to cater for demand, a figure which if achieved would make them third biggest rice producer in the world, behind only China and India.

Similarly, if the Japanese then decided to wash down their rice with the same quantity of beer as sumos (6 pints or 3.4 litres per meal, or 12 pints/6.8 litres a day) it would see Japan go from being the 34th biggest consumer of beer in the world per capita to the runaway leader with a total that was more than the rest of the top 30 countries' total consumption combined.[8]

But what if every man in the UK aspired to be a *rikishi*? And, more importantly, what would be the consequences if every adult male decided, *en masse*, to eat like one, too?

Clearly the impact of such a shift in eating habits would be truly seismic. Certainly, the face of sport in the nation would change immeasurably. After the unparalleled sporting success of the summer of 2012, a wholesale change in training methods as gargantuan as this would have serious repercussions and leave many questions requiring answers. For example, would 152 lb (69 kg) Bradley Wiggins' bike collapse if he suddenly trebled in weight? How would Andy Murray reach those drop shots with 350 lb (158 kg) of extra weight to carry around the tennis court? And would a 500 lb (226 kg) David Beckham still model underwear?

A case in point here is the sport of motor racing and particularly Formula 1, where former world champions Jenson Button and Lewis Hamilton would no longer be able to race in the event. Why? Because strict F1 regulations dictate "a driver must be able to get in and out of the car without removing anything other than its steering wheel. Once strapped into the car with all his safety gear on, he must be able to remove the steering wheel and get out within five seconds, and then replace the steering within a further five seconds."[9] Of course, a sumo with a waistline of over 50 inches (127 centimetres) won't be able to get into the car, let alone get out of it in five seconds. That said, as both drivers are no longer resident in the UK – Button now lives in Monaco and Hamilton in Switzerland – they may be exempt from the new diet.

Although the idea of our sporting heritage being cast asunder by a new generation of gluttons suddenly incapable of competing might be amusing, the wider implications of a nation of sumo-style eaters may not be so comical. While it may appear that there would be a huge economic fillip for the likes of farmers and food retailers, haulage contractors and manufacturers of oversized clothing, the reality would be that almost everything in everyday life would need to be modified, altered or even radically redesigned. New and bigger vehicles, from motorbikes to cars to vans, would be needed to accommodate the fuller figures of male drivers. In 2011, for example, the average waist size of a British man was 35.8 inches (90 cm)[10] but the waistline of an average sumo wrestler can extend well beyond 46 inches (117 cm), a figure that also means the seating capacity on all forms of public transport would be significantly reduced as well.

And the downsides don't end there. Though there would be hundreds of thousands of new jobs created by the huge additional demand for food and clothing, whether or not you could find fit and able men to carry them out would be another matter entirely. The security of the nation could also suffer.

Anybody who wants to train to be a pilot in the Royal Air Force, for instance, cannot be more than 213.18 lb (96 kg) in weight[11], while those wishing to enlist in Her Majesty's Armed Forces must have a Body Mass Index (BMI) of between 18 and a maximum of 32.[12] To put that into some of kind of context, a sumo wrestler standing 5'11" (1.8 m) tall and weighing 400 lb would have a BMI reading in excess of 55.

Meanwhile, the nation's welfare bill, for so long a perennial political hot potato, would be brought into even sharper focus as the myriad complaints associated with morbid obesity see absenteeism from work increase and claims for incapacity and disability benefits soar. The National Health Service would cease to function as the wide range of ailments and diseases that sumo wrestlers suffer from, ranging from high blood pressure to hypercholesterolaemia, cardiac arrests to arthritis in their joints, place a burden that is too much to withstand. The fact that there would also be a concomitant shortage of male staff in the hospitals merely serves to compound the issue.

One of the most likely complaints to afflict those on a sumo diet would be Type 2 diabetes. In the UK, there are currently around 2.9 million diabtetes sufferers, with another apparently 850,000 as yet undiagnosed.[13] Ninety per cent of these suffer from Type 2 diabetes. In 2010/11, the cost of Type 2 diabetes (both in terms of treatment and the effect on the economy) was an estimated £21.8 billion ($35 billion) per year, with patient care accounting for £8.8 billion ($14.1 billion) and indirect costs such as illness, absenteeism and informal care making up the remaining £13 billion ($20.9 billion). Moreover, deaths from diabetes resulted in over 325,000 lost working years.[14]

The consequence, then, of all of the men in the UK adopting a sumo diet would see an increase in these costs to the point where not only would the NHS collapse overnight, but the country would be bankrupt too. With 20,979,401 men in the 15–64 age bracket in the United Kingdom[15] and three men being diagnosed with Type 2 diabetes for every two women[16], we can estimate that the predicted cumulative costs (direct and indirect) of Type

2 diabetes attributable to poor diet and obesity would rocket to £175 billion each year, or about four times what the UK spends on defence annually.[17]

One of the few consolations, if it could be deemed as such, is that savings might then be made in many areas, simply because the life expectancy of a sumo wrestler is 10 years less than that of regular males in Japan.[18] Applied to the United Kingdom, this would see the average man live to just 68.1 years rather than the current 78.1 years[19]. Theoretically, this could save some £2,000 ($3,220) in annual Winter Fuel Payments and £55,874 ($89,557) in state pensions per adult male of pensionable age.

That said, coffins would cost more, too.

NOTES & SOURCES

1. *www.telegraph.co.uk/earth/earthnews/9345086/The-worlds-fattest-countries-how-do-you-compare.html.*

2. *weightlossresources.co.uk.*

3. *World Bank, 2011*

4. *faostat.fao.org*

5. Japan Times, *January 2012*

6. *factsanddetails.com/japan*

7. *www.riceassociation.com*

8. *Kirin Institute of Food and Lifestyle Report Vol. 33, Global Beer Consumption by Country in 2010*

9. *www.formula1.com.*

10. *British Heart Foundation survey, October 2011.*

11. *www.army.mod.uk/aviation/18096.aspx.*

12. *www.army.mod.uk/documents/general.*

13. *www.nhs.uk.*

14. *www.nhs.uk/news/2012/04april/Pages/nhs-diabetes-costs-cases-rising.aspx.*

15. *United Kingdom Demographics Profile, 2012 (www.indexmundi.com).*

16. *'Estimation of the Prevalence of Diagnosed Diabetes from Primary Care and Secondary Care Source Data', J.N. Harvey, L. Craney, D. Kelly,* Journal of Epidemiology & Community Health *2002; 56 18–13.*

17. *Total UK defence spending in 2012 was £45.8 billion, www.ukpublicspending.co.uk*

18. *www.japantoday.com.*

19. *www.statistics.gov.uk.*

28. DECISIONS, DECISIONS...
Just who would be a referee or an umpire?

It's the very definition of a thankless task: a job so stressful and so heavily scrutinised that every decision you make can have a huge impact, not just on the encounter at which you're officiating but quite possibly on a player's – and coach's – career, or a team's entire season.

Yes, being a referee or an umpire is a remarkably tough job, irrespective of what sport you're working in and, indeed, what level you're operating at.

Do your job and do it well, and nobody will even mention it. Make one bad call, though, and suddenly you'll be the centre of unwanted attention. In 2009 for example, the Football Association (FA) estimated that around 20 per cent of the lowest-level matches in England took place without an appointed referee simply because they could find no one willing to endure the 90 minutes of abuse, while in 2010–11, the *Yorkshire Post* revealed FA statistics showing that there had been some 330 assaults on referees in football at that level during the season (up from 260 the previous season), while 276 cases actually amounted to common assault.[1]

Given the incessant verbal abuse and the threat of physical assault, why would anyone ever want to become a referee? Well, on the one hand there is doubtless the sense of power that being in control inevitably brings, while on the other there's the chance that if your career in officiating really takes off, then there could be a very nice living to be made from doing the job.

Take English football's Premier League, for instance, where following the establishment of the 'Select Group' of officials in

2001, a collection of some 16 referees (including the man who refereed the 2010 World Cup Final, Howard Webb) were given full-time contracts for the first time in the domestic game. Appointed by the Professional Game Match Officials Board (PGMOB), each of these referees is now paid a reported annual salary of over £70,000 ($112,000) per year,[2] where once they had been paid a fee for each game that they oversaw. It's not exactly a life of penury for those officials or assistant referees who are not part of the Select Group either: for each Premier League game at which they officiate, they receive £600 ($966) plus overnight accommodation.

But as the game itself has become more professional, so too has the need for the match officials to follow suit and the modern-day elite referee now has to endure the kind of training that may have felled his predecessor. Twice a year they are required to undergo strict fitness tests, while every fortnight the Select Group convenes not just to gain detailed analysis of their most recent performances, but also to receive useful advice from everyone involved in the game, from podiatrists to sports psychologists.

It was shown that Select Group referees taking charge of Premier League matches get 92 per cent of key decisions correct, while their assistants get 99.3 per cent right.

It's an approach that seems to have garnered some remarkable results. Despite ceaseless in-depth analysis of their performance and, more specifically, their mistakes, the Select Group can point to some extremely convincing statistics to show just how effective the well-paid professional match official is. In recent studies compiled by match assessors working for the Professional Footballers' Association and League Managers Association, it was shown that Select Group referees taking charge of Premier League matches get 92 per cent of key decisions correct, while their assistants get 99.3 per cent right.[3]

In tennis there is a similar elite band of officials – the 26 gold badge umpires – who officiate at the Grand Slam events and the more high-profile tournaments on the ATP World Tour and WTA circuits. In 2011, gold badge umpires received £189 ($304) per day at Wimbledon, while the French Open paid £153 ($246) per day and the Australian Open paid £245 ($394) per day worked, with overtime on offer if the umpire worked in excess of 10 hours on a given day. The US Open, meanwhile, was the least well paid of the four Grand Slam events, paying £156 ($251) for each main draw game worked and £115 ($185) per day for every qualifying match.[4]

And just as Premier League referees are given accommodation as part of their contract, the gold badge umpires are entitled to a variety of expenses. Though each Grand Slam event is different, umpires typically receive meal vouchers worth between £15 ($24) and £23 ($37) each day and at the French and US Opens they also receive private rooms for accommodation, with shared rooms on offer at the Australian Open. At Wimbledon, the organisers prefer umpires to make their own arrangements, instead giving them a stipend of £80 per day to cover costs. Travel expenses are also covered in part at each of the Grand Slams, with around £312 ($500) to £623 ($1,000) (US) on offer to umpires.

Increasingly, even those sports that have never really entertained the idea of full-time professional match officials have been forced to concede the benefits of having dedicated referees. In Australian Rules Football's AFL, the 98 elite umpires can earn more than £65,245 ($105,000) a season and this despite holding down full-time jobs in their professional lives. Recently, however, discussions have taken pace between the AFL and the umpires' union, the Australian Football League Umpires Association, to explore the possibility of a new group of professional elite referees being formed, one where they no longer have to juggle the demands of the sport with those of their day job.[5]

There is no such issue in some of the big American sports, however, where the referees and umpires are paid the kind of salaries that would be the envy of most professional sportsmen and women across the globe. In basketball's NBA, for example, entry-level referees can expect to earn £93,000 ($150,000) per season, while the most senior officials earn significantly more. In 2009, this was £342,788 ($550,000) a year, or £93,481 ($150,000) more than the US President is paid annually.[6] But then even the mascots in the NBA make £25,000–£28,000 ($40,000–$45,000) a year.[7] Similarly, there are some startling salaries to be made in Major League Baseball (MLB), but only when umpires have reached the top. When they work in the minor leagues, baseball umpires earn around £1,120 ($1,800) a month, but by the time they make it to MLB, they can earn as much as £186,000 ($300,000) annually, with an additional £212 ($340) worth of allowances for every game at which they officiate and baseball's regular season comprises of 162 games.[8]

In the NFL there are 121 referees whose average pay in 2011 was £94,000 ($150,000). While this may seem a generous remuneration, it's but a small percentage of the revenues gleaned by the NFL.

But if the officials in baseball and basketball are sitting pretty, there's a growing sense of injustice among referees in the National Football League (NFL). In the NFL there are 121 referees whose average pay in 2011 was £94,000 ($150,000). While this may seem a generous remuneration, it's but a small percentage of the revenues gleaned by the NFL. In 2011 this amounted to some £5.8 billion ($9.3 billion), a figure expected to climb to over £7.5 billion ($12 billion) in the very near future. It also turned out to be a bitter pill for the referees who, keen to secure a better deal for themselves and a bigger pension pot, decided to withdraw their labour at the start of the 2012 season, leaving the NFL games to be refereed by replacements.[9]

Across all sports, though, there is now a clear trend of governing bodies establishing 'elite' groups of officials in recognition, perhaps, of the need for the highest possible standards in what are increasingly lucrative competitions, and where there is simply too much at stake to leave it in the hands of the ill-equipped. While many sports have chosen to assist their officials with technology, few have made as great a play of using it as cricket, where the umpires have to stand and maintain their concentration for up to seven or eight hours a day. Here the use of such innovations as Hot Spot, Hawk-Eye and the Snickometer in their Umpire Decision Review System (DRS) has proved an invaluable tool for the International Cricket Council's (ICC) 12-strong select group of umpires – the Emirates Elite Panel of Referees (yes, it's even sponsored) – not because it makes their job easier but because it helps eradicate some of the doubt associated with certain decisions.

Not that the Elite Panel has to work that hard. No, on average each elite umpire can stand in 8–10 Test matches and 10–15 one-day internationals (in addition to any ICC World Events) in any given year, which gives them a potential annual workload of 75 days plus travel and preparation time.[10] The fact that they also receive £4,100 ($6,600) per Test match and £2,050 ($3,300) per one-day international *and* a yearly retainer as well, must surely make it one of the best part-time jobs ever.[11]

NOTES & SOURCES

1. When Saturday Comes, *October 20, 2011.*
2. *www.guardian.co.uk/football/2012/apr/14/premier-league-referees-no-excuses*
3. The Observer, *April 14, 2012.*
4. *Former ATP Tour pro Mike Plantz (www.quora.com).*
5. *www.theage.com.au, January 28, 2011.*
6. *www.whitehouse.gov.*
7. *Raymond Entertainment Group – providers of NBA mascots.*
8. *CNN, October 2009.*
9. *www.guardian.co.uk, September 12, 2012.*
10. *www.icc-cricket.com.*
11. The Herald Sun, *February 12, 2008.*

29. GOLDEN MEMORIES
When sports memorabilia collecting turns into colossal cash ...

For some it's a hobby, for others it's an investment. For a few it's a livelihood, while for some people it's the key to a vast fortune. This is sports memorabilia, a world where a football player's sock or an ice hockey puck can mean serious money and where one man's tat is another's treasure.

But what constitutes memorabilia and what makes it valuable? Well, the popularity and collectability of a particular piece can be determined by a number of factors. Some will be items that have become valuable for a specific reason or a defining moment in the sport's history, or what's often referred to in the industry as "game-used" – the baseball that wins the World Series, the football that secures the World Cup, the cricket bat that broke all records. But by and large, it is those pieces that not only have historical significance but also a celebrity provenance, such as the pieces belonging to a sports star whose celebrity has crossed into the mainstream – Babe Ruth or Muhammad Ali, for example – that seem to become eminently more collectable and therefore valuable on the open market. In such cases, an autographed item with a certificate of authenticity will significantly increase a piece's value but an autographed piece dedicated or addressed to a particular person will not be quite so collectable.

Today, though, there is a second string of memorabilia – manufactured memorabilia, if you like – wherein sports stars are paid by dealers to autograph goods so that these can then be sold on to fans for a significant profit. A day after the New York Yankees' Derek Jeter made his 3,000th hit in July 2011, for example, he spent a day at the HQ of sports memorabilia company Steiner Sports, signing 500 baseballs and 400 photographs – items that Steiner then sold on for £434 ($699.99) for the balls and between £372 ($599.99) and £495 ($799.99) for the photos. That said, some athletes actually devalue their items by signing too many things, making their autograph and therefore the piece in question less collectable on the open market.[1]

Rarity or scarcity is also important in determining the value of an item. For example, a New York Yankees' jersey worn by Lou Gehrig only in away games which sold for £227,000 ($365,000) in 1992 – and is now said to be worth in the region of £466,000 ($750,000) – will always be worth more than a similar, more commonly found shirt because so few are in existence. And if the legendary athlete happens to be no more, all the better.

Some athletes actually devalue their items by signing too many things, making their autograph and therefore the piece in question less collectable on the open market.

The baseball example is a useful case in point because it remains the sport that dominates the upper echelons of the memorabilia market. Indeed, baseball-related artefacts account for 14 of the 20 most expensive sales of sporting collectables, with 25 per cent of the list made up by Babe Ruth memorabilia. And while there would appear to be little historical difference between, say, the shirt that Pelé wore in Brazil's 1970 World Cup Finals and a uniform worn by Babe Ruth (in fact, you might argue that Pelé's shirt is globally more recognisable), the US obsession with the self-styled 'Sultan of Swat' means that Ruth's jersey will fetch a figure running into millions of dollars while Pelé's shirt will go for a fraction of that price. Indeed, the last time Pelé's shirt from the 1970 World Cup Final was auctioned, at Christie's in 2002, it sold for 'just' £157,500, or around $250,000.[2]

THE MOST EXPENSIVE SPORTS COLLECTABLES

How sweaty old kit, used equipment and throwaway cigarette cards came to be worth millions.

BABE RUTH'S JERSEY – £2.75 MILLION ($4.4 MILLION)

Not just any old jersey but the Sultan of Swat's earliest one in existence, having worn it for the New York Yankees in his first season after the switch from the Boston Red Sox.

THE ORIGINAL RULES OF BASKETBALL – £2.6 MILLION ($4.2 MILLION)

The very documents put together by James Naismith that codified one of the world's most popular sports. They were sold at auction for twice the price they were expected to achieve.

MARK MCGWIRE'S 70TH HOME RUN BALL – £1.8 MILLION ($3 MILLION)

This record-breaking ball, originally retrieved by a fan in the crowd, research student Philip Ozersky, was later sold by him at auction for three times the guide price.

BABE RUTH'S BAT – £0.8 MILLION ($1.3 MILLION)

The bat with which the Babe hit a home run on the day the Yankee Stadium opened: April 18, 1923. Its value was also increased by the fact that it was autographed by Ruth.

HONUS WAGNER BASEBALL CARD – £0.75 MILLION ($1.2 MILLION)

One of the first five members of the Baseball Hall of Fame, this card of the Pittsburgh Pirates' shortstop dates back to 1909 and is known by its series name, the T206.

MUHAMMAD ALI'S BOXING GLOVES – £0.68 MILLION ($1.1 MILLION)

The very gloves that the legendary boxer wore in his heavyweight title fight with Floyd Patterson in Las Vegas, November 1965.

BABE RUTH SALE CONTRACT – £618,633 ($996,000)

The original legal document exchanged between the Boston Red Sox and the New York Yankees when Babe Ruth switched teams in 1920.

BABE RUTH WORLD TOUR UNIFORM 1934 – £478,881 ($771,000)

A uniform worn by Babe Ruth during an off-season tour to Japan; the value was improved enormously by its excellent condition.

HANK AARON'S 755TH HOME RUN BALL – £403,726 ($650,000)

In 1976, Aaron's final home run of his career also set the all-time home record of 755 and this ball was grabbed by one of the Milwaukee Brewers ground crew. When he refused to give it back, the Brewers fired him.

SHOELESS JOE JACKSON'S BAT – £360,258 ($580,000)

Known as the "Black Betsy", this is the only "Shoeless" Joe Jackson signature model thought to be in existence.

Sources: www.bornrich.com, sports.yahoo.com.

NOTES & SOURCES

1. The New York Times, *July 15, 2011.*
2. The Telegraph, *April 27, 2002.*

30. ULTIMATE ACHIEVEMENTS
We watch sport to see history made but what is the rarest feat in sport?

The Crucible Theatre, Sheffield, England... It's the 1983 World Championship and after 15 reds, 15 blacks and five of the final six colours, Cliff Thorburn is one last pot away from recording the first-ever televised maximum break of 147 at snooker's World Championship. As the Canadian addresses the white ball, running his cue between thumb and index finger, the BBC commentator, 'Whispering' Ted Lowe, is only too aware of what might be about to happen. "Oh, good luck, mate!" he says in hushed tones. Moments later, Thorburn rolls the black into the corner pocket and drops to his knees in celebration, the crowd in raptures behind him.

Thorburn's televised maximum break was the first at the Crucible and, following Steve Davis's 147 at the Lada Classic in Oldham of 1982, only the second on TV. At the time of writing, 30 years on, there have been 96 maximum 147 breaks in professional tournament snooker and although still relatively rare, barely a competition goes by where a player doesn't roll one in or come very close. That, certainly, is a sure sign that the standard of the game has improved massively since the days of Thorburn's prime. Even the speed at which the players achieve the maximum break is faster. When Thorburn made his maximum in 1983 it took him over 15 minutes to compile. When Ronnie O'Sullivan made his 147 at the World Championship in 1997, it took him just five minutes and 20 seconds.[1]

And yet the 'maximum break' tag is actually a misnomer as it is, theoretically at least, possible to make a break of 155 in snooker. For example, if a player breaks off at the beginning of a frame but makes a foul to leave his opponent 'snookered' on all of the 15 red balls, the other player is entitled to take a 'free ball', which counts as an additional red ball (worth one point) and then take another colour after it. If this was a black ball (worth seven points), and he followed it up with 15 reds, 15 blacks and the six colours – yellow (two points), green (three), brown (four), blue (five), pink (six) and black (seven) – he would amass a break of 155.

While nobody has made a break of 155, there has been one notable example of a player making a break in excess of 147 in tournament play. In October 2004, during the qualifying rounds for the UK Championship in Prestatyn, Wales, the Scottish player Jamie Burnett became the first player in history to record a competitive break of more than 147 when he scored 148 against Leo Fernandez. Taking a brown as a free ball, he then potted the brown again, followed by the 15 reds with 12 blacks, two pinks, a blue and the final six colours.[2]

Yet the 'maximum break' tag is actually a misnomer as it is, theoretically at least, possible to make a break of 155 in snooker.

What's for sure is that the 147 or more break is still one of sport's ultimate achievements, but in a world where many sports have similarly rare feats, where does it stand? And, moreover, how do you determine which achievement is the hardest? While the obvious way is to simply compare how many times a given feat has occurred, this fails to take into account how much opportunity the participants have to actually achieve it. A pitcher in Major League Baseball, for example, theoretically may have around 180 games over the course of one season to throw a 'perfect game', while a bowler in Test match cricket may have only a dozen or so Test matches, or a maximum of 24 innings, in which to take all 10 opposition wickets.

There has to be a line drawn as to what actually constitutes the 'ultimate achievement', too. While a player scoring 50 goals or more in a soccer season or a running back rushing 2,000 yards (1828 metres) in the course of an American football season may be rare and, indeed, impressive, these are self-imposed, self-determined and man-made conceits – targets that, in reality, might just as well be scoring 45 goals or rushing 2,012 yards (1840 metres). It's the same in professional golf, when commentators and statisticians talk about how many 'Top 10' finishes players have had. The truth is, they could just as well say how many 'Top 13' finishes. In the grand scheme of things, it means nothing.

The feats we will examine here will be those that simply cannot be bettered. That's to say, the maximum scores that a participant can achieve in a given sport in a given situation. It's the rarity value coupled with sublime skill, and the fact that the opposition is powerless to do anything about it, that elevates these achievements to near-legendary status. For some of these feats, there is nothing to prevent the exponents from reaching such highs other than the extent of their own talent. In golf, arguably one of the most solitary sports of all, there is just the golfer against the course; whereas in snooker, there is an opponent, but if you're at the table, potting balls, there's nothing he can do about it. And in darts, where the nine-dart finish is the perfect way to win a game, it's you against the dartboard irrespective of who you're playing.

Let's take darts, where there have been 34 televised nine-dart finishes since the sport first came on to the small screen in 1975. Today, it's England's 16-time World Champion Phil 'The Power' Taylor who leads the way, with nine 9-darters to his credit, including two in the same match against James Wade in the Premier League on May 24, 2010.[3] Though there are many ways to achieve a nine-dart finish, the most common way is to begin with two maximum scores of 180 (three x treble 20) before completing the outshot with the last three darts. For this to happen, the player will usually have to throw eight darts in succession into an area that is just 8 mm wide, followed by a double that is still 8 mm wide but only slightly longer, and all from the regulation throwing distance of 2.37 metres (7' 9¼").[4]

As a sporting achievement it ticks virtually all of the boxes: accuracy, concentration, skill, technique... The only thing it doesn't really require is physical fitness.

The same might be said of golf too, and while it's tempting to look at the game and consider how difficult it is to achieve a hole-in-one, the very fact that there were 37 on the European Tour[5] and 35 on the PGA Tour during the 2012 season[6] suggests that it's not exactly a rare occurrence. Moreover, it is not something that golfers consciously set out to do, and it relies not just on a well-executed shot but on elements of good fortune too. In that respect, then, another benchmark must be examined. So, in terms of something that cannot be attributed to luck and clearly demonstrates consistent skill over time, it's perhaps more apt to look at the incidence of rounds of golf that have taken under 60 shots.

The 'sub-60' round in competition is the holy grail of golfers. While there have been 26 rounds of 60 in PGA Tour tournament golf, the first occurring in 1951 when Al Brosch hit one in the third round of the Texas Open, the number of players to have gone one crucial shot or more better is significantly lower. Yes, there have been recorded scores as low as 55, but in terms of ratification by *Guinness World Records* these do not count as they were either played in non-tournament golf or on courses of less than 6,500 yards (5,943 metres) in length. But in official tournaments on major tours there have been 11 rounds of 59 and one of 58. The latter, by Ryo Ishikawa in the Crowns event on the Japanese Tour of 2010, remains the lowest official round in history, although two other scores of 58 – by Ishikawa's compatriot Shigeki Maruyama in a qualifying round for the US Open in 2000 and the American Jason Bohn in the Bayer Championship on the minor Canadian Tour of 2001 – have also been made. Interestingly, there has never been a sub-60 round on the European Tour.

Again, the problem here is with the courses that have been used. Some are nearly 8,000 yards (7,315 metres) long, others 2,000 yards (1,838 metres) shorter. Some have high rough and innumerable bunkers, while others have wide-open spaces and generous greens; some are set up with low scores in mind whereas others have devilish pin positions. A case in point is how the United States Golf Association (USGA) set up their courses for the US Open. With tight fairways, punitive rough and treacherous greens, the winning score (save for a few exceptions such as Rory McIlroy's record-breaking score of -16 at Congressional in 2011) is rarely in the high under-pars and often a few shots over-par. Contrast that with the Open Championship in Britain, where for the last three times that the competition has been staged at St Andrews, the home of golf, the winning scores have been -16, -14 and -19. Yes, the truth is that some golf courses are just much easier than others, which makes the

But if apparently non-athletic sports like darts, snooker and golf may be considered, so too can ten-pin bowling, where the perfect "300-point game" is regarded as the pinnacle of the sport.

quest for the sub-60 round entirely reliant not just on the course you're playing on but on the way it's been set up and, of course, variables such as the weather too.

But if apparently non-athletic sports like darts, snooker and golf may be considered, so too can ten-pin bowling, where the perfect '300-point game' is regarded as the pinnacle of the sport. To achieve 300 points, a bowler must bowl 12 'strikes' in a row (a strike occurring when all 10 pins are knocked over in one single delivery), with one strike in each of the first nine frames and then three in the concluding tenth frame. In many respects, the 300-point game is similar to the nine-dart finish in that both require unnerring accuracy, with tiny margin for error. In darts, a player can hit the wire of the board and the dart may bounce out, or he can flick off the barrel of one of his previous darts, thereby diverting the dart from its intended target. In ten-pin bowling, meanwhile, the slightest discrepancy in your entry angle or even the position of your feet on delivery can ruin the chances of a perfect game. That said, the 300-point game is actually very common among professionals and amateurs alike. In the Professional Bowlers Association (PBA) in the US, there have been 22 on national television alone and more scores that were either on the cable channels or simply not broadcast at the time.[7]

The notion then of a 'perfect game' is something that you, the participant, have complete control over, regardless of the opposition or any other variables. In that respect, the perfect game in baseball – where a pitcher throws through all nine innings and achieves victory without any of the opposition batsmen ever reaching base (the so-called '27 up, 27 down') – ranks highly, especially as only 23 pitchers have achieved it in Major League Baseball history. The most recent was the Seattle Mariners' Félix Hernández in a game against the Tampa Bay Rays on August 15, 2012.[8]

The notion then of a 'perfect game' is something that you, the participant, have complete control over, regardless of the opposition or any other variables.

What's intriguing is the point at which sports stars realise that something extraordinary is about to happen. Snooker players often say that they knew a 147 "was on" after three or four pots, simply because of the way that the balls had spread around the table. Similarly, batsmen in cricket don't set out to hit six sixes in one over but once the first two or three deliveries have sailed over the boundary, the temptation to try and add your name to a very short list is often too great to resist.

Famously, it was Nottinghamshire's West Indian all-rounder Garry Sobers who first achieved this, bludgeoning Glamorgan's Malcolm Nash all around the ground in a county match in Swansea in 1968. Since then, only three other men have achieved this feat in first-class cricket: Ravi Shastri for Bombay in 1985, Herschelle Gibbs (South Africa) in 2007 and Yuvraj Singh for India, also in 2007. But as with golf and the variation in the size and set-up of the courses, so the standard of the wicket and whether it has been prepared with batsman or bowler in mind can also weigh heavily in favour of one side or the other.

The other factor, of course, is the quality of the opposition and their bowler. In the case of Gibbs' achievement, for instance, he was facing the international minnows Holland and their leg-spinner, Daan van Bunge. Even Nash of Glamorgan had decided to bowl slow left-arm spin instead of his usual medium-pace seam bowling when Sobers took him to task in 1968.[9]

There is one sporting achievement, one piece of perfection, that seems to be if not in a league of its own then somewhere close to it: the so-called 'golden set' in tennis. Superficially, winning 24 consecutive points (or not conceding any) may not seem to be the 'ultimate achievement' but what makes it so is that it not only allows for no errors whatsoever from the player striving to do it, but also assumes that at no stage in those six games will his opponent manage to hit a single winning shot either. In snooker's 147 or the nine-dart finish in darts, for example, you live or die by your own efforts and nothing your opponent does can stop you from achieving your goal. In tennis, however, there are too many variables – double faults, lucky net cords, bad line calls and so on.

To date, there have been but three golden sets in the history of professional tournament tennis: Pauline Betz v. Catherine Wolf in Cincinnati, Ohio (1943), Bill Scanlon v. Marcus Hocevar (1983) and Yaroslava Shvedova v. Sara Errani in 2012. However, Shvedova's golden set stands out as the only one to be made in the history of the sport's four majors, the Grand Slams. It happened at the 2012 Wimbledon Championships in London when the Kazakhstani won the first 24 points in her third-round match against Italy's Errani, but what made Shvedova's golden set even more intriguing was that she almost achieved the same feat in 2006 in a tie against Amy Frazier in Memphis, Tennessee. Having taken 23 straight points from the start and raced to 5-0 and 40-0, Shvedova then double-faulted on her serve. What happened next was scarcely believable. Though she managed to win the first set 6-1, Shvedova then lost the next two 6-0, 6-0 and her dream of a golden set turned into a nightmare that she would rather forget.[10]

NOTES & SOURCES

1. *news.bbc.co.uk/sport1/hi/other_sports/snooker/2968373.stm.*
2. *'Burnett's Break Goes One Better',* Guardian, October 18, 2004.
3. *Unicorn: The Big Name in Darts,* Unicorn Darts News section, May 24, 2010.
4. *darts501.com.*
5. *www.europeantour.com.*
6. *pgatourmedia.pgatourhq.com.*
7. *news.pba.com/post,* March 4, 2012.
8. *'Felix Hernández Pitches Perfect Game as Seattle Mariners Beat Rays',* Guardian, *August 1, 2012.*
9. *www.espncricinfo.com.*
10. *'Unseeded Shvedova Achieves Golden Set at Wimbledon',* Independent, *June 30, 2012.*

31. WEIGHTY ISSUES
Why there are relatively few slim darts players...

People participate in amateur sport for many reasons: for fun and enjoyment, general wellbeing and also for the camaraderie. But for those who are playing sports to lose weight, it is an area fraught with innumerable, often contradictory messages.

So while bodies such as the American College of Sports Medicine and the American Heart Association both recommend that a person wishing to lose weight performs 60 to 90 minutes of physical activity each day,[1] there's an increasing amount of scientific evidence to suggest that exercise has only a negligible effect when it comes to weight loss.

In the United States, for example, leading medical research centre the Mayo Clinic[2] found that "an exercise regimen is unlikely to result in short-term weight loss beyond what is achieved with dietary change." That is to say, if you cut back a little on certain foods then you're just as likely to lose weight as you are by exercising. Yes, exercise can make a diet more effective but on its own it is unlikely to produce the kind of results people may expect or have been led to believe. To prove that theory, in 2009 Dr Timothy Church of the University of Louisiana conducted a study of 464 overweight women who either did no exercise at all or were given a personal trainer for 72, 136 or 194 minutes of supervised exercise over a period of six months[3]. When the study period had elapsed, Church found that the women who exercised the most did not lose the most weight and that some women in each of the four groups even gained 10lb (4.5kg) or more.

At the Pennsylvania State University, meanwhile, another study compared groups of men on 12-week programmes of either diet alone, or diet combined with exercise of 50 minutes three times a week.[4] The result showed that those men who dieted and exercised lost an average of just a single pound more than the ones who didn't have to visit the gym.

The issue, it seems, is not so much with the kind of exercise people do (as all forms of exercise will burn calories, albeit at varying rates) but their expectations as to what it will do to their body and how long it will take to achieve the desired results. Yet losing just 1 lb (0.45 kg) in body weight takes more time and effort than you might imagine. While it seems like a comparatively small amount of weight to shed, it's the equivalent of around 3,600 calories, which means that in order to lose that pound you have to burn 3,600 calories more than you take in. If you run at a moderate pace for half an hour a day you can expect to lose it in around eight days, but if you're planning on doing it by playing darts you could be looking at three weeks of traipsing up and down the oche before you finally lose it.

While 1 lb seems like a comparatively small amount of weight to shed, it's the equivalent of around 3,600 calories, which means that in order to lose that pound you have to burn 3,600 calories more than you take in.

It is also about the response to the exercise after people have trained or worked out. For some, the end of a workout is cause for celebration, a moment to reward yourself with a treat or two for all the effort you've just put in (even though it will take you around half an hour of swimming to burn off a Mars bar). If you like, it's compensation for the exertion. It's here, though, that good intentions are cast asunder because while exercise can help aid weight loss in conjunction with a diet, it also stimulates hunger and increases appetite. And therein lies the problem. The more you exercise, the hungrier you

SPORTS AND THE CALORIES THEY BURN

Based on the following, it's easy to understand why darts players have fuller figures.

Exercise/Activity	Calories Used
Running	450 calories (per 30-minute run at 8-minute mile pace)
Football	900 calories per hour
Squash	816 calories per hour
Tae Kwon Do	700 calories per hour
Boxing (Sparring)	612 calories per hour
Basketball	600 calories per hour
Cycling	598 calories per hour
Tennis	600 calories per hour
Lacrosse	544 calories per hour
Swimming	500 calories per hour
Cricket	340 calories per hour
Golf	306 calories per hour
Volleyball	272 calories per hour
Table Tennis (Ping Pong)	272 calories per hour
Sitting Down Playing with the Kids	197 calories per hour
Darts	170 calories per hour

Note: Above figures are based on amateur participants weighing 150lb (68kg) and performing at moderate intensity.

Sources: www.sports.yahoo.com, www.caloriecount.about.com, www.dietandfitnesstoday.com and www.nutristrategy.com.

will become and the more you eat, the more exercise you need to do to shift it.

You just can't win.

Notes & Sources

1. *Physical Activity and Public Health Updated Recommendation for Adults From the American College of Sports Medicine and the American Heart Association, August 2007.*
2. *www.guardian.co.uk/lifeandstyle/2010/sep/19/exercise-dieting-public-health*
3. *'Effects of Different Doses of Physical Activity on Cardiorespiratory Fitness Among Sedentary,Overweight or Obese Postmenopausal Women With Elevated Blood Pressure A Randomized Controlled Trial,' Dr Timothy Church, 16 May, 2007*
4. *Influence of Exercise Training on Physiological and Performance Changes with Weight Loss in Men,' William J. Kraemer, Jeff S. Volek, Kristine Clark, Scott E. Gordon, Susan M. Puhl, L. Perry Koziris, Jeffrey M. McBride, N. Travis Triplett-McBride, Margo Putukian, Robert U. Newton, Keijo K Häkkinen, Jill A. Bush, Wayne J. Sebastianelli. Department of Kinesiology, Noll Physiological Research Center, The Pennsylvania State University, 1999.*

32. FAR AND AWAY
The long and the short of away fixtures

In this age of astronomical wages and multi-million pound contracts, it's not unusual to see the occasional ostentatious display of wealth among the football fraternity. While one might forgive the occasional lapse from a young player who suddenly finds himself thrown into a life of luxury and is unable to cope with his new-found fame and fortune, for the football clubs themselves such behaviour might be viewed as unacceptable.

In October 2012, Arsenal FC travelled the 100 miles (160 km) or so to their away fixture at Norwich City, not by team coach or by train but by plane, and their flight from Luton Airport to Norwich Airport took just 14 minutes to complete. Of course, many in the game viewed the trip as a total extravagance, not least because (a) they left on the day before the game, and (b) if you added together the time it took to drive the 31 miles (50 km) from the club to Luton Airport and then factored in the check-in process, time spent reclaiming baggage and the additional five-mile (8 km) journey from the airport to Carrow Road, it would have taken just as long to drive from London to the match. Not that it did them any good – they still lost 1-0.

Moreover, some expressed concern about the environmental impact of taking such a short flight, with an estimated tenth of a tonne of carbon emissions produced for each and every person on the return trip.[1] If we assume that the club's party amounted to, say, 30 people, that would mean Arsenal would have to plant roughly six trees to offset the carbon produced from flying to East Anglia for their match.

Arsenal's decision to fly such a short distance looks to have been an oversight, and seems at odds with some of the club's environmental protection initiatives. These even include their 2012/13-season kit being made from recycled polyester[2].

The environment and a team's impact on it can no longer be ignored, and one club taking a lead is baseball's Philadelphia Phillies. In 2007, the team had made (unwanted) history in becoming the first-ever professional sports franchise to lose 10,000 games. The following year, however, the Phillies took the unprecedented step of buying 20 million kilowatt-hours of Green-e Energy Certified Renewable Energy Certificates – sufficient to offset an entire year of power usage for the team and a move that was the environmental equivalent of planting 100,000 trees. Later that year, the newly-green Phillies went on to win baseball's biggest prize: the World Series. Was it karma? Who knows, but at least the Phillies won with a clean conscience.

Of course not all professional football clubs have the wherewithal to travel to away fixtures by air. For those cash-strapped clubs in the lower leagues, who simply cannot afford to take to the skies, inevitably this means taking to the road and this can make for some mind-numbingly long journeys. In English football, the longest journey between two league clubs is that taken by Plymouth Argyle in Devon to Carlisle United in Cumbria. While the two clubs are at the time of writing in different divisions, over the years they have often played each other and at 389.2 miles (623 km) by road, the distance between the two grounds remains the longest possible trip you can make in English football. For the record, it should take six hours and 30 minutes (roadworks permitting)[3], but produces just 18.8 kilograms of CO2.

This, however, is but a short hop on a bus for some of the other teams around the world. In Australia's A-League, there is even a game referred to as 'The Distance Derby' such are the huge distances involved for the two participating clubs. Contested by Perth Glory and the New Zealand club Wellington Phoenix, it's a match that requires one club to travel some 3,270 miles

(5,232 km) just to fulfill the fixture. In this case, of course, it is impractical for either club to take anything other than a plane to reach the other side's ground, but the clubs based in mainland Australia do at least have the option of an alternative means of transport if they're keen to reduce their carbon footprint. When Western Australia's Perth Glory take on Queensland's Brisbane Roar, for instance, they have three options available to them. Were they to take the team bus and drive the 2,711-mile (4,337 km) journey, it would take almost two days. Alternatively, they could take the train but that would involve a 65-hour trip on the Indian Pacific line just to reach Sydney, where they would

In Australia's A-League, there is even a game referred to as "The Distance Derby". Contested by Perth Glory and the New Zealand club Wellington Phoenix, it's a match that requires one club to travel some 3,270 miles (5,232km).

then have to change to board another train north to Brisbane, a journey that would take an additional 14 hours. The flight from Perth International Airport to Brisbane Airport, meanwhile, takes around five hours.

They have similar distances to negotiate in North America, where the many franchises in basketball and baseball, American football and ice hockey all have to endure similar East to West coast travel arrangements. In the National Football League (NFL), Florida's Miami Dolphins have to make a 2,722-mile (4,355 km) trip to play the Seattle Seahawks, while in the NHL the Vancouver Canucks must make a near 5,300-mile (8,480 km) round trip when they play the Florida Panthers.[4]

But the journeys involved in the A-League and in the mainstream US sports pale into insignificance when compared to the plight of one club in Russia. As the world's biggest country, it is inevitable that Russian clubs will face away fixtures that involve significant distances, but no club in the world faces the same sort of travel trouble as Vladivostok's Luch-Energiya must endure. Situated in the far south-east of Russia, not far from the border with North Korea, Luch-Energiya's nearest club – their rivals, if you like – are SKA-Energiya Khabarovsk, who are based some 500 miles (800 km) away or, to put it another way, the same as if Swindon Town were to play Scotland's Inverness Caledonian Thistle as a local derby.

The remoteness of Luch-Energiya's location presents many problems for the club, especially as the vast majority of professional teams in Russia are situated in the west of the country. A case in point came in the 2009 season when they were drawn against the Baltic seaport club of Baltika Kaliningrad in the Rambler Cup competition. This would be a tie that involved a round trip for the team and their fans of around 9,000 miles (14,490 km) through eight time zones. It was hardly surprising. After all, Vladivostok, where Luch are based, is actually closer to Australia than it is to Kaliningrad. Small wonder that the team were once actually sponsored by the Aussie lager, Castlemaine.

A tie that involved a round trip for the team and their fans of 9,150 miles (14,640 km) through eight time zones!

Of course, the beauty of sport is that not only do most competitions involve a home and an away fixture (meaning the opposition do some of their share of the travelling, too), but, Luch-Energiya aside, you're just as likely to face a short trip as a long haul to a fixture. While there are many clubs, such as AC Milan and Internazionale at the San Siro and Roma and Lazio at the Stadio Olimpico, who share grounds, there are other clubs whose grounds are so close to each other that it would be quicker for a team to walk to their rivals' ground than take the team coach. In England, for example, Nottingham Forest's City Ground is around 300 yards (274 metres) away from the ground of their rivals Notts County, Meadow Lane; whereas the distance between Liverpool's Anfield ground and the stadium of their long-standing rivals Everton at Goodison Park is about half a mile. It's in Scotland, though, where the UK's closest professional grounds lie. In Dundee, a city of

A LONG WAY TO FLY TO LOSE

The longest away round trips and their impact on the environment if you travel by air.

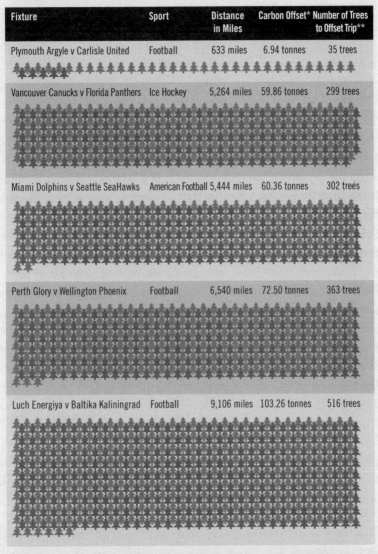

Fixture	Sport	Distance in Miles	Carbon Offset*	Number of Trees to Offset Trip**
Plymouth Argyle v Carlisle United	Football	633 miles	6.94 tonnes	35 trees
Vancouver Canucks v Florida Panthers	Ice Hockey	5,264 miles	59.86 tonnes	299 trees
Miami Dolphins v Seattle SeaHawks	American Football	5,444 miles	60.36 tonnes	302 trees
Perth Glory v Wellington Phoenix	Football	6,540 miles	72.50 tonnes	363 trees
Luch Energiya v Baltika Kaliningrad	Football	9,106 miles	103.26 tonnes	516 trees

Note: Travel calculations based on 50 players/club representatives travelling. Tree offset calculation is based on a tree planted absorbing one tonne of CO2 over its lifetime; but as trees grow, some may die or be destroyed and not all will achieve their full carbon offset potential. In light of this, this calculator assumes that five trees should be planted to ensure that at least one lives to 40 years or that their combined carbon offsetting equals one tonne.
Sources: www.travelmath.com, www.carbonify.com/carbon-calculator.

TRULY LOCAL RIVALRIES

Cheap to get to, but there's no escaping rivals – and neighbours' banter – if your team loses.

Fixture	Sport	Distance	Walking time*
Manchester United v Man City	Football	4 miles	77 minutes
Everton v Liverpool	Football	0.6 miles	12 minutes
Nottingham Forest v Notts County	Football	0.2 miles	5 minutes
BKV Elore v MTK (Budapest)	Football	0.05miles	1 minute
AC Milan v Internazionale**	Football	0 miles	0 minutes

*based on average walking speed of 3.1 mph
**AC Milan and Internazionale share the same stadium

just 140,000 people, they have two Scottish Premier League teams – Dundee and Dundee United – whose stadiums, Dens Park and Tannadice, are but 200 yards (183 metres) apart. Yet that distance seems like a marathon if we look further afield. In Budapest, Hungary, for instance, there are two teams, BKV Elore and MTK, whose grounds are separated by only a small street, while in Argentina the stadia of Independiente and Racing Club – The Estádio Juan Domingo Perón and The Estadio Libertadores de América – sit right next to each other in Avellaneda, Buenos Aires. They're so close, in fact, that they are literally a kick of a ball away.

NOTES & SOURCES
1. *www.carbonadvicegroup.com.*
2. Metro, *July 12, 2012.*
3. *www.theaa.co.uk.*
4. *wwwsportmapworld.com.*

33. SHOW ME THE MONEY!
Do professional footballers really earn that much money?

Footballers' wages, or rather the sheer size and scale of them, is one of those perennial bugbears that football fans often discuss over a post-match pint when they are dissecting a match. Ever since the introduction of the breakaway FA Premier League in 1992 and the boom fuelled by Sky Sports' investment in the new division, the players have enjoyed an unparalleled prosperity, where even the less gifted among them can become multi-millionaires.

To put that rise into some kind of perspective, it's worth looking at what players would have earned in years gone by. In January 2011, the Professional Footballers' Association (PFA) released a report highlighting the difference between the wages of players of today and those paid to their counterparts in years gone by[1]. They estimated that an England international playing for a top club like Manchester United in 1957 would have earned a total of £1,677 ($2,699) in wages, bonuses and match fees each year, a sum that in today's money would have been the equivalent of around £75,000 ($120,000) per annum – or what many Premier League players now earn in just one week.

But it's football's top earners whose salaries draw the most opprobrium. Today, salaries in excess of £100,000 ($160,000) per week are routine, while those in excess of £200,000 ($320,000) are becoming increasingly common.

An interesting example is Manchester United striker Wayne Rooney, who moved to Old Trafford from Everton in the summer of 2004 and went from being an £80-a-week ($120) trainee to a millionaire overnight. Further new contracts and salary increases have followed and in 2010 United's board signed off on a new contract for the England international worth a reported £250,000 ($400,000) per week.[2]

While the size of Rooney's new deal made the headlines – it had made him the best-paid player in the Premier League – unlike his off-field earnings, it is subject to the same Pay As You Earn taxation as any other regulation employee. In itself that makes for some extraordinary results in that each month he would pay income tax of £539,843.83 ($869,148.56) and have an additional £21,944.78 ($35,331.09) taken in National Insurance contributions. Annually, it would amount to combined stoppages of £6,741,463.36 ($10,853,756), leaving Rooney with a net annual wage of £6,258,536.64 ($10,076,244), or nearly half a million pounds less than his total stoppages.[3]

While Wayne Rooney's weekly wage is perhaps atypical of Premier League footballers – the average weekly wage is just £22,353 ($35,998) – it does show the earning potential of the best and most high-profile players.

But then Rooney's off-field earnings more than help to make up for whatever he loses in tax and National Insurance and it was a much-publicised court case in February 2010, when Rooney was sued by his former management company, the Formation Group and Proactive Sports Management, that revealed the extent of his true earning potential. According to the papers that were originally filed in 2008, Rooney made an additional £760,000 ($1,223,600) every six months for his image rights at Old Trafford, £1 million a year from Nike to wear and promote their boots and £118,869 every six months from the computer games company, EA Sports. He also earned £3.5 million from a 12-year, five-book contract with HarperCollins Publishers and £600,000 from a four-year arrangement with Coca-Cola.[4]

While Rooney's weekly wage at Manchester United is perhaps atypical of Premier League footballers – the average weekly wage is just £22,353 ($35,998) – it does show the earning potential of the best and most high-profile players. The lower you slide down the leagues, however, the greater the disparity in salaries. In 2010, the average weekly salary of a player in the second tier Championship was £4,059 ($6,534), while players in the third tier, League One, received an average weekly salary of £1,410 ($2,270). Players in League Two, the fourth tier, had a weekly salary of just £747 ($1,202), which is not much more than the UK's national average.

Indeed, such has been the growth in the top flight in the last 20 years, all fuelled by some stratospheric TV rights deals, that in 1992, just before the FA Premier League came into being, the average wage in the top flight was around £1,152 ($1,854) a week, or 3.8 times the average wage in the then lowest tier, the Third Division. By 2012, the difference had grown to 30 times.[5]

In 2010, the average weekly salary of a player in the second tier Championship was £4,059 ($6,534), while players in the third tier, League One, received an average weekly salary of £1,410 ($2,270).

Of course, it's a similar story across Europe, where salaries at the big clubs like Real Madrid, Barcelona and Bayern Munich stand comparison with the biggest clubs in the UK. However, in the less high-profile top-flight professional leagues in Europe the salaries lag some way behind. In Belgium's Jupiler League, for example, a player earned an average of just €210,000 (around £180,000/$290,000) a year during the 2010–11 season.[6] Put another way, that's around two-thirds of what Wayne Rooney earns in a single week.

But it was ever thus. The bigger clubs attract the bigger fan base, the bigger fan base attracts the bigger money, and the bigger money attracts the bigger players. And therein lies the problem. As with any sport, or indeed entertainment industry, it's those players and performers who bring something unique to the table, the ones who draw supporters to the stadium, that can command the highest salaries and while this, in turn, increases the average salary of those who perhaps don't boast the same star quality, it also serves to increase the pay gap between those who haven't yet reached the higher echelons of their sport.

Moreover, in the modern age where billionaires treat football clubs like their own personal playthings, the size of a star player's salary seems to be without limit. Take the Cameroonian striker Samuel Eto'o, who left Italy's Internazionale in August 2011 to join the Russian side Anzhi Makhachkala. Owned and funded by the billionaire Suleyman Kerimov, the club has aggressively sought to bolster both its team and coaching staff in recent years with some high-profile recruits, including their coach, the former Dutch national manager Guus Hiddink. Eto'o, meanwhile, was lured to Russia by a contract that paid him a reported £18 million ($29 million) *after* tax each year, or around £350,000 ($560,000) a week.[7] It was a contract that made him not just the world's highest-paid footballer but also the highest-paid individual in any team sport in the world. But then we shouldn't have been surprised by Kerimov's generosity. After all, when the Brazilian full-back Roberto Carlos celebrated his 38th birthday at the club, Kerimov treated him to a €1.8 million Bugatti Veyron as a little present.

> **The contract paid Eto'o a reported £18 million after tax each year... It made him not just the world's highest-paid footballer but also the highest-paid individual in any team sport in the world.**

But football, or soccer, is not alone and there are several sports that eclipse it in terms of average salaries. Baseball, for example, boasts 16 of the top 20 most lucrative contracts ever awarded in sport with only Eto'o (at number one), Real Madrid's Cristiano Ronaldo (10), F1's Kimi Räikkönen (15) and Barcelona's Lionel Messi (18) interrupting the sport's dominance. In 2011, the average annual salary of the 844 players in Major League Baseball on opening-day rosters was £2.13 million ($3.44 million), up 4.1 per cent from 2010, while the team with the highest average salary, the New York Yankees, paid each of their

THE ANNUAL SALARY OF AN FOOTBALLER

Compared to the average UK salary, considerable financial rewards are on offer to players in football's top division. However, lower league footballers receive relatively little for such a short career.

1984–85 FOOTBALL SEASON

Average UK salary: £9,894
First Division: £24,934
Second Division: £15,507
Third Division: £11,507
Fourth Division: £8,314

1992–93 FOOTBALL SEASON

Average UK salary: £18,356
Premier League: £77,083
First Division: £40,728
Second Division: £21,840
Third Division: £16,640

2001–02 FOOTBALL SEASON

UK Average salary: £27,300
Premier League: £566,932
First Division: £115,700
Second Division: £50,336
Third Division: £28,600

2009–10 FOOTBALL SEASON

UK Average salary: £34,112
Premier League: £1,162,350
Championship: £211,068
League One: £73,320
League Two: £38,844

Note: Numbers shown indicate basic pay only and excludes appearance money and bonus payments.

Sources: Professional Football Association, (Football League figures), Sportingintelligence.com (Premier League figures since 1992)

players an average of £4,175,756 ($6,722,968).[8] Of course, this average was so high because the Yankees paid their third baseman Alex 'A-Rod' Rodriguez £20 million ($32 million) a year, pitcher CC Sabathia £15,084,294 ($24,285,714) a year and first baseman, Mark Teixeira, £14,363,354 ($23,125,000) a year, but it does demonstrate just how well paid other sports can be, given a wide enough market and genuinely mass appeal.

But it's that other staple of the American sports fan's diet, basketball, that commands the highest average salaries and in 2010, the players in the NBA received an average salary of £3.468 million ($5.585 million), making them the highest-paid athletes in any team sport in the world, more even than the players in the National Football League (NFL). They may play for some of the richest franchises in sport – 32 of the top 50 highest-valued teams or franchises are from the NFL – but their wages are less, on average, than those in the NBA ranks.

Of course, such huge salaries are not limited to sport and it's common for the likes of captains of industry, best-selling music stars and A-list actors to take home equally if not more impressive pay packets. The chief executive of the Goldman Sachs banking group, Lloyd Blankfein, enjoys a £1.24 million ($2 million) basic salary, a £1.86 million ($3 million) cash bonus and a total package of £10 million ($16.2 million)[9], while the world's highest-earning pop star of 2011 was the Irish band U2[10], who made a reported £121 million ($195 million). In Hollywood, meanwhile, it's the actor Tom Cruise who commands the highest fee for his films and in 2011–12 he reportedly made £46 million ($75 million) from appearing in blockbuster movies such as *Mission: Impossible – Ghost Protocol.*[11]

But while the salaries of Hollywood's A-listers compare favourably with the likes of Wayne Rooney, the wage packets of the most popular television actors in the UK do not, even though they perform to many more million people, each and every week. *Coronation Street*, for example, is, like United, based in Manchester and the TV programme commands a cumulative audience each week of 41.49 million viewers[12], whereas Manchester United's total attendance for the entire 2011–12 Premier League season was just 1,432,358.[13] While Rooney is United's highest-paid player, the highest-paid actor on *Coronation Street* is reportedly William Roache (who plays the character of Ken Barlow). Coincidentally, he too earns £250,000 – only unlike Rooney's salary, this figure is annual.

NOTES & SOURCES

1. *www.telegraph.co.uk/sport/football/competitions/premier-league/8265851/How-footballers-wages-have-changed-over-the-years-in-numbers.*

2. The Sun, *October 24, 2010.*

3. *www.listentotaxman.com.*

4. *www.dailymail.co.uk/news/article-1247995/Rooney-Coleen-sued-4-3million-exploited-agent.html.*

5. *www.dailymail.co.uk/sport/football/article-2055140/Premier-League-wages-FIVE-times-Championship.html.*

6. *www.epfl-europeanleagues.com/pro_league_average_earnings.htm.*

7. *www.dailymail.co.uk/sport/football/article-2028746/Samuel-Etoo-set-worlds-earning-player-350-000-week-Anzhi-deal.html.*

8. *Associated Press, April 5, 2011.*

9. *Reuters, April 13, 2012.*

10. *www.forbes.com.*

11. *www.guardian.co.uk, July 4, 2012.*

12. *BARB, w/e October 28, 2012.*

13. *www.soccernet.espn.go.com.*

34. FOOD FOR SPORT
The economics of spectator snacks and the humble matchday pie

Matchday catering has always suffered a bad press. From the terrace days of hot Bovril burning the roof of your mouth to the hot dogs and hamburgers of dubious provenance, the fare on offer for the average football fan was often ghastly and never gourmet.

But there is one dish that has remained constant in the live football experience, a reliable and satisfying savoury snack that stands proud amid a menu of mediocrity. Yes, the humble pie holds a very special place in the heart, mind and stomach of the British football fan. For many, a game without one is like the Tower of London without the ravens, or Queen playing on without Freddie Mercury – it's just wrong.

As a matchday snack, the pie takes some beating. Substantial enough to satisfy but portable enough to be consumed standing up or on the move (and without cutlery, too), its compact design fits perfectly with the demands of the hungry football supporter, eager to see the game. Certainly, the popularity of the pie shows no sign of abating, even in the face of some stiff competition in the market from relative newcomers such as pasties and pizza slices.

In the 2011/12 season it's estimated that around two million pies were sold at British football grounds. One manufacturer, Leicestershire's Pukka Pies, supplies over 700,000 pies to 40 football clubs in the Premier League and Football League during the season. In 2010/11, their research showed that Rotherham United was the club where the most pies were sold per capita, with 40 per cent of those in attendance at the club's Don Valley ground buying one on matchdays. Typically, though, only around 15–20 per cent of the crowd will buy a pie on a matchday[1], but even if you take the lower estimate it would still mean that 11,371 people of a full house at Manchester United's Old Trafford would buy one and the revenue from those sales alone would be over £35,000 ($56,000) which, coincidentally, is the amount Wayne Rooney gets each day to play for United.[2]

But there are regional variations in the pre-match preferences of football fans, too. In the Midlands and South, for example, the most popular flavour is steak and kidney, while in the North and Northwest the pie of choice tends to be meat and potato.[3] Increasingly, though, more exotically-flavoured pies are appearing on the club menus, to the point where the Indian-influenced chicken balti pie now ranks third in popularity behind the classic meat or steak pie and other chicken-based varieties.[4]

Only around 15–20 per cent of the crowd will buy a pie on a matchday, but even if you take the lower estimate it would still mean that 11,371 people of a full house at Manchester United's Old Trafford.

The rise of the Chicken Balti pie has been phenomenal. Introduced at Aston Villa and Walsall by Shire Foods in 1997, they are now sold at over 70 clubs, with Shire producing over 100,000 a month to cater for demand. The thinking behind the pie was inspired. "In the Nineties the Midlands was famous for balti meals," says Shire's Vic Doyle. "As a pie manufacturer we thought it was a great opportunity. A typical Friday night for many young males is lager and a curry, so we thought if you get all that in the authenticity of a pie product, it would work at football."[5]

As the balti boom illustrates, the culinary taste of the average football fan is changing and clubs have to adapt to accommodate their fans. Thirty years ago, all a vegetarian supporter could hope to buy from the catering stand was perhaps a packet of crisps or maybe a Kit Kat. Today, however, there is a much greater awareness and appreciation of the dietary needs and preferences of the fans in the stands and while meat pies, in all their many guises, continue to be the matchday market leader, the fact that clubs like Brighton & Hove Albion now offer an award-winning butternut squash and coriander pie at their new American Express Community Stadium, while Arsenal sell a roasted vegetables and cauliflower pie is proof, perhaps, of a growing shift in tastes away from the tried, tested and more traditional tastes.

In 2012, Premier League Aston Villa even managed to use their new pie as a force for good in helping to raise awareness of leukaemia. When their midfielder Stiliyan Petrov was diagnosed with the disease, the club and its supporters rallied round in support of the popular Bulgarian international and soon afterwards, a limited edition pie containing chicken, leek and Bulgarian kefta meatballs was launched, with the proceeds going to the Cure Leukaemia charity.[6]

It's also apparent that football clubs have never been more willing to experiment with new and interesting items on the matchday menu, which, sacrilegious though it may sound, are not pies. In the 2011/12 season, for instance, Manchester City began selling 'The Manchester Egg', which, for the uninitiated, is a boiled egg encased in black pudding and then deep-fried. Invented by amateur chef Ben Holden, the snack had been such a success at the Manchester Food and Drink Festival that it was soon on sale at the Etihad Stadium.[7]

But that kind of innovation has also found favour outside of the stadia, with the popularity of some clubs' matchday snacks now being presented to an entirely different audience to the one for which they were originally intended. Football League Two club Morecambe FC's steak and ale pie and their chicken, ham and leek pie are so good that they're now even stocked 250 miles away in Harrods. But while fans at the club's Globe Stadium pay £2.50 ($4) for their matchday snack, Harrods' customers have to fork out £9.95 ($16) for the privilege of enjoying theirs.[8]

While the pie-eyed punters at Harrods may have to dig a little deeper than those at the Globe Stadium, there are still some significant disparities in the amount that clubs charge their supporters to enjoy one. Generally speaking, the further south you travel, the more expensive the pie becomes. So if you watch your football in Scotland, you can get a pie for just £1 at Division Two clubs such as Alloa Athletic, Forfar or Albion Rovers; and if you're heading for a game at Accrington Stanley in Lancashire you can have one for £1.50. But by the time you get to Fulham in west London or Brighton & Hove Albion on the south coast you're looking at £3.90 for one (unless you opt for the discounted 'Pie and a Pint' deal for £7.00). Strangely, it's not the same pattern with hot drinks, though, where you can buy a cup of tea at Stevenage (Hertfordshire) or Crawley (West Sussex) for as little as a £1, but when you head to the North West and the two Manchester clubs, City and United, you'll have to hand over £2.50 for a cuppa. Having said that, the milk and sugar are complimentary.[9]

Over the course of the All-England Championships, fans will work their way through 28,000kg of strawberries, served up with over 7,000 litres of fresh cream.

But food is a key part of the live sport experience, whatever sport it is you choose to watch. Like football in the UK, the pie, or more specifically, the meat pie, is also the staple snack for spectators at Australian Rules Football and at Australian cricket matches too. But in sports like tennis, the popularity of food seems to depend on the location of the tournament. At Wimbledon, for instance, the tradition of eating strawberries with cream is particular only to SW19. Over the course of the All-England championships, for instance, fans will work their way through 28,000kg of them, served up with over 7,000 litres of fresh cream.[10]

Similarly, at professional golf tournaments, the snacks differ from event to event. At the Masters, for instance, not only is the food some of the cheapest on offer at any major sporting event – an egg salad sandwich is just 93 pence ($1.50) and a beer just £1.86 ($3) – but their signature Piemento Cheese sandwich (also

93 pence/$1.50) is now as much part of the patron's Augusta experience as watching the winner slip on the Green Jacket.[11]

At Major League Baseball, meanwhile, it is the hot dog that is the snack of choice at the ballparks. In 2011, for example, it was estimated that 22,435,400 hot dogs were sold across MLB in the season[12] or, to put it another way, enough hot dogs that if they were laid end-to-end would stretch from Great American Ballpark in Cinncinnati all the way to the AT&T Park in San Francisco.

The League's biggest dog fans, meanwhile, are at the LA Dodgers, where two million of them are sold each season, followed by the New York Yankees (1.2 million) and the Philadelphia Phillies (1.5 million). What is interesting about the Dodgers record, though, is that it could be argued that it is significantly more than two million hot dogs per season as one of their most popular varieties is the 'Dodger Dog' which is actually a foot-long frankfurter and therefore significantly bigger than standard hot dogs.

NOTES & SOURCES

1. *Peter Mayes, Pukka Pies, interview on www.guardian.co.uk, January 27, 2010.*
2. The Sun, *October 24, 2010.*
3. *www.pukkapies.co.uk/pukka-news.php.*
4. *Ibid.*
5. *'Matchday Feeding – How Chicken Balti Pie Became a Cult',* Observer, *August 12, 2007.*
6. *The EurosportAsia, April 20, 2012.*
7. Daily Mail, *November 3, 2011.*
8. The Sun, *June 14, 2012.*
9. *"The Price of Football",* BBC Sport website survey, August 2012.
10. *www.wimbldeon.com*
11. *www.augusta.com*
12. *National Hot Dog and Sausage Council's 2011 annual report*

35. THE SPORT'S THE MOVIE STAR
And will snooker be the sports film subject of the future?

One of the constants of modern cinema is the sports movie, and hardly a month goes by without there being a major film release that draws its storyline or background from a popular sport or sporting event.

Sports movies have the potential to be the year's biggest revenue earners and their mainstream subject matter means they're always contenders for film awards, but making a compelling and authentic film about sport is one of the most difficult tasks to confront a director. Sports fans, with their attention to detail and encyclopedic knowledge, will typically seize on any opportunity to expose flaws and faults in a film that fails to accurately portray their team or their favourite player, or gets key facts and figures wrong.

For aficionados, the crucial issue is often how accurately the action scenes are shot. In *Rocky*, Sylvester Stallone's Oscar-winning boxing picture from 1976, the fight sequences perfectly complemented the narrative and highlighted the agony that the eponymous lead and, more importantly, his partner, Adrian, suffered during the denouement. Watch 2002's *Bend It Like Beckham*, however, and the manner in which the star, Keira Knightley, toe-pokes the football around the pitch is so unrealistic as to render the whole film and its otherwise interesting premise more than a little ridiculous.

Yes, when they get it right, as Martin Scorsese did with his boxing epic *Raging Bull* in 1980, it makes for the kind of movie that entertains, inspires and lives long in the memory. But when they get it wrong, as they did in 2004 with the widely panned tennis-based romantic comedy *Wimbledon,* it makes for the kind of experience that leaves cinema-goers heading for the exits.

But while the staples of the sports film genre continue to be mainstream activities like American football, baseball, football and boxing, it's true to say that no sport is truly exempt from the keen-eyed scriptwriter. Indeed, virtually every game imaginable has at some time been used in a movie plot. From lawn bowls (*Blackball,* 2003) to rugby league (*Up 'n' Under,* 1998), lacrosse (*Crooked Arrows,* 2012) to pool (*The Hustler,* 1961 and *The Color of Money,* 1986), if there's a story lurking behind the action then the directors will find a way of telling it.

Sport, then, remains extremely fertile ground for moviemakers. Almost every week, somewhere in the world, there is another epic tale of peerless heroism unfolding in the world of sport, where good overcomes evil, or triumph kicks tragedy firmly into touch. The key, as with any good movie, is the story itself. It's not enough for a team to simply overcome the odds and win. There needs to be a rollercoaster of a journey along the way, where relationships are tested and heartstrings tugged. They don't always have to win in the end – *Rocky* being a prime example – but as long as personal pride is restored and a tear or two shed along the way, it's likely to be a surefire hit at the box office.

From lawn bowls to rugby league, lacrosse to pool, if there's a story lurking behind the action then the directors will find a way of telling it.

As with sport itself, there is no certain formula for box-office success, however by studying past successes in the film genre and looking for future trends, a producer can increase his chances of a hit. The world's largest movie market[1] is the United States and Canada, grossing £6.36 billion ($10.2 billion) in 2011, and as a result movie producers major on North American sports. Of the 120 top-grossing sports films released since 1976[2] American football has been the subject of 26 films, baseball 22 and basketball 16, while boxing has been the star of 15. Boxing has generated the most revenue per film release of any sport (£1.34 billion/$2.16 billion) and this is largely due to the highly-successful *Rocky* franchise (four of its films are in the top ten highest-grossing sports movies, see page 204) and shows how one successful movie can spawn many others – that is until viewers tire of unlikely ageing boxer comebacks.

While these numbers indicate that it is logical to have your film based on popular sports, a number of minority sports make an appearance in the 120 top sports movies. The minor sport of dodgeball was the star of a 2004 movie and generated £83 million ($134 million) at the US box office. Even arm wrestling, largely thanks to Sylvester Stallone at the height of his fame, was featured as the subject of a successful film called *Over the Top* (1987).

Of course, tastes change, and so does the movie audience, and it is predicted that by 2020 North America will no longer be the world's largest film market, having been overtaken by China.[3] This information will not have been lost on film producers and as a result, the sports movie of the future may be a little different and instead feature China's most popular sports. You can expect more basketball movies, as it is China's most popular sport[4], but don't be surprised if soon your local multiplex is also showing movies of other sports with a massive Chinese following, such as table tennis, badminton or even snooker![5]

Whatever the sport, the sports movie is here to stay and as Gordon Gray, the man who produced such acclaimed sports dramas as *The Rookie* (baseball, 2002) and *Invincible* (American football, 2006) once suggested, "Sports films are really just chick flicks for guys."

THE TOP 10 HIGHEST-GROSSING SPORTS MOVIES

1. ROCKY (United Artists, 1976)
Sport: Boxing
Starring: Sylvester Stallone
Tagline: "His whole life was a million-to-one shot."
US Domestic Gross: £73 million ($117 million)
Adjusted for Inflation (2011): £283 million ($456 million)

2. ROCKY III (United Artists, 1982)
Sport: Boxing
Starring: Sylvester Stallone
Tagline: "A Fighter. A Lover. A Legend. The Greatest Challenge."
US Domestic Gross: £78 million ($125 million)
Adjusted for Inflation (2011): £178 million ($286 million)

3. HEAVEN CAN WAIT (Paramount, 1978)
Sport: American football
Starring: Warren Beatty, James Mason and Julie Christie
US Domestic Gross: £50 million ($81 million)
Adjusted for Inflation (2011): £172 million ($277 million)

4. THE BLIND SIDE (Warner Bros, 2009)
Sport: American football
Starring: Quinton Aaron, Sandra Bullock
Tagline: "Based on the extraordinary true story."
US Domestic Gross: £159 million ($256 million)
Adjusted for Inflation (2011): £166 million ($267 million)

5. ROCKY IV (United Artists, 1985)
Sport: Boxing
Starring: Sylvester Stallone
Tagline: "He could have stopped the fight. He could have saved his best friend's life. But now, the only thing he can't do is walk away."
US Domestic Gross: £80 million ($128 million)
Adjusted for Inflation (2011): £163 million ($263 million)

Source: www.imdb.com

6. ROCKY II (United Artists, 1979)
Starring: Sylvester Stallone
Tagline: "There is one fight left. He must win it with his hands ...
she must win it with her heart."
US Domestic Gross: £53 million ($85 million)
Adjusted for Inflation (2011): £161 million ($260 million)

7. THE KARATE KID PART II (Columbia, 1986)
Sport: Karate
Starring: Pat Morita, Ralph Macchio
Tagline: "The story continues ..."
US Domestic Gross: £71 million ($115 million)
Adjusted for Inflation (2011): £144 million ($232 million)

8. THE WATERBOY (Buena Vista, 1998)
Sport: American football
Starring: Adam Sandler
Tagline: "Instant Hero. Just add water."
US Domestic Gross: £100 million ($161 million)
Adjusted for Inflation (2011): £139 million ($224 million)

9. JERRY MAGUIRE (TriStar Pictures, 1996)
Sport: American football
Starring: Tom Cruise, Cuba Gooding Jr.
Tagline: "The journey is everything."
US Domestic Gross: £95 million ($153 million)
Adjusted for Inflation (2011): £135 million ($217 million)

10. THE LONGEST YARD (Paramount, 1974)
Sport: American football
Starring: Burt Reynolds, Eddie Albert
Tagline: "First down ... and 10 years to go."
US Domestic Gross: £27 million ($43 million)
Adjusted for Inflation (2011): £120 million ($193 million)

The Top 120 Movies by Number of Releases and Revenue

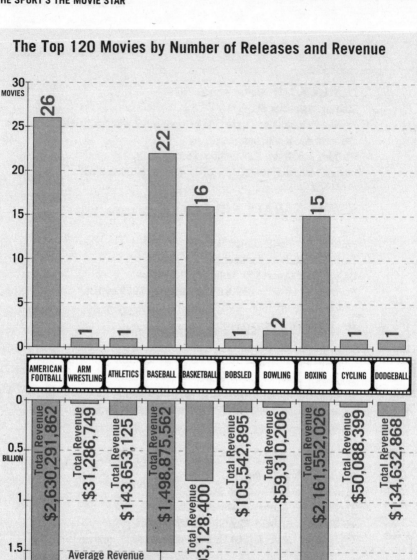

MOVIES

30
25
20
15
10
5
0

26 — AMERICAN FOOTBALL
1 — ARM WRESTLING
1 — ATHLETICS
22 — BASEBALL
16 — BASKETBALL
1 — BOBSLED
2 — BOWLING
15 — BOXING
1 — CYCLING
1 — DODGEBALL

BILLION

0
0.5
1
1.5
2
2.5
3

Total Revenue $2,630,291,862
Total Revenue $31,286,749
Total Revenue $143,653,125
Total Revenue $1,498,875,562
Total Revenue $793,128,400
Total Revenue $105,542,895
Total Revenue $59,310,206
Total Revenue $2,161,552,026
Total Revenue $50,088,399
Total Revenue $134,632,868

Average Revenue Per Movie: $68,130,707

Average Revenue Per Movie: $49,570,525

Average Revenue Per Movie: $29,655,103

Average Revenue Per Movie: $144,103,468

Average Revenue Per Movie: $101,165,071

Source: www.imdb.com

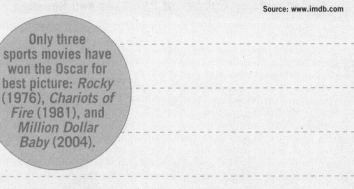

Only three sports movies have won the Oscar for best picture: *Rocky* (1976), *Chariots of Fire* (1981), and *Million Dollar Baby* (2004).

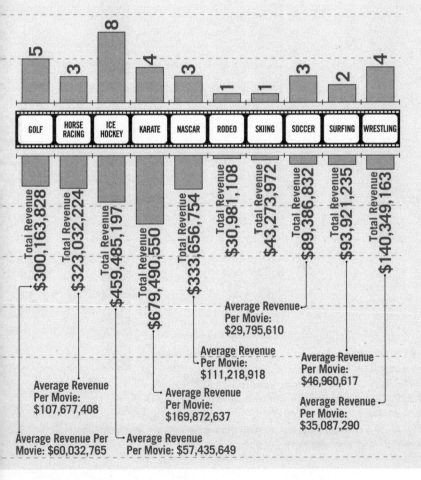

5	3	8	4	3	1	1	3	2	4
GOLF	HORSE RACING	ICE HOCKEY	KARATE	NASCAR	RODEO	SKIING	SOCCER	SURFING	WRESTLING

Total Revenue $300,163,828

Total Revenue $323,032,224

Total Revenue $459,485,197

Total Revenue $679,490,550

Total Revenue $333,656,754

Total Revenue $30,981,108

Total Revenue $43,273,972

Total Revenue $89,386,832

Total Revenue $93,921,235

Total Revenue $140,349,163

Average Revenue Per Movie: $29,795,610

Average Revenue Per Movie: $111,218,918

Average Revenue Per Movie: $46,960,617

Average Revenue Per Movie: $169,872,637

Average Revenue Per Movie: $35,087,290

Average Revenue Per Movie: $107,677,408

Average Revenue Per Movie: $60,032,765

Average Revenue Per Movie: $57,435,649

NOTES & SOURCES

1. *Motion Picture Association of America.*
2. *ww.imdb.com.*
3. *www.latimes.com/entertainment/envelope/cotown/la-et-ct-china-largest-movie-market-20121128,0,4904380.story.*
4. *www.latimes.com/entertainment/envelope/cotown/la-et-ct-china-largest-movie-market-20121128,0,4904380.story.*
5. *www.chinadaily.com.cn/sports/2010-04/06/content_9691844.htm.*

ACKNOWLEDGEMENTS

First, I'd like to thank my editor, Matt Lowing, who is one of the most patient and understanding people I've ever had the pleasure of dealing with.

I'd also like to thank two people who helped shape my formative years and gave me some of the knowledge to wade through the facts, stats and numbers I encountered researching this book. So a heartfelt thank you to my old secondary school maths teacher, Dennis Winters, and my economics teacher at sixth-form, Mike O'Hare. They say you never forget a great teacher and these men really were the best in the business.

Thanks to friends, colleagues and sports fans like Mark Leigh, Neil Smith, Tim Southwell, Iesytn George, Danny Crouch, Alexis James, Mike Herd, Dan Davies, Paul Henderson, Mark Addison, Paul Bradford, Matt Adams, Joe Butler, Andrew Woods, Mike Harris, Alex Narey and anyone else who knows me. A special word of thanks should also be reserved for Tom Brown, who, despite being a Manchester United fan, has also been a source of advice, support and inspiration.

On the family front, I'd like to thank Mum, Dad and Darren for their continued support and Betty Farragher for all her encouragement. Thanks also to the three small people that bring me fun, laughter and, for the time being, child benefit – Betsy, Frank and Cissy. Finally, thanks to my beautiful and loving wife Ann, who puts up with me through these difficult times, bringing me bread and wine as I toil.

INDEX

100 metres
speed in 47–54
Aaron, Hank 168
Abbondanzieri, Roberto 128
Abrahams, Harold 52
AC Milan 43, 127, 129
Accrington Stanley 198
achievements in sports 169–76
Adams, Nicola 28
age of sportspeople 21–6
Ainslie, Ben 151
Akers, Nick 17
Akhtar, Shoaib 89
Albion Rovers 198
Ali, Muhammad 168
Allen, Mark 109
Alloa Athletic 198
American Express Community Stadium 16
American football
away fixtures in 183
colours in 44–5
commentators in 86
easy games in 141
fastest throw 92
injuries in 134, 135
intelligence in 106–7
movies about 203, 204, 205, 206
referees in 162
America's Cup 144
animal sports 65–8
Anzhi Makhachkala FC 190
Araújo, Ronny Heberson Furtado de 90
arm wrestling
movies about 206
Arsenal 16, 33–4, 129, 139, 181, 182, 197
Ashes urn 145
Ashley, Mike 15
Aspandiyarova, Dina 38
Astle, Jeff 32
Aston Villa 196, 197

athletics
movies about 206
Australian Rules football
and birth dates 66–7
umpires in 161
away fixtures 181–6
Ba, Demba 128
badminton
shuttlecock speed 91, 92, 93
Bailey, Donovan 53
Balitika Kaliningrad FC 184, 185
ball sports
fastest 89–94
injuries in 135
Balla, Ibrahim 38
Bangladesh 141
Barcelona FC 123, 127, 129
Barkley, Charles 86
Barnes, John 88
Barrow, John 49
Barston, Peter 118
Barton, Robert 42, 43
baseball
achievements in 170, 174
ball speed 89–90, 92
catering in 198–9
colours in 44
earnings in 192
injuries in 135
memorabilia 165–6, 167, 168
movies about 206
naming stadiums 16, 19
referees in 162
basketball
calories burnt 179
commentators in 86
earnings in 192
injuries in 132, 135
memorabilia 167
movies about 206
naming stadiums 18
referees in 161–2

Basque Pelota
ball speed 92
Bayern Munich 43, 127, 129
Beckham, David 95–102, 125, 155–6
Bend It Like Beckham 201
Benfica 43
Betz, Pauline 175
Bieber, Justin 111, 113
birth dates
and sporting success 11–14
BKV Elore FC 186
Black, Roger 88
Blaszczykowski, Jakub 128
Blatter, Sepp 74
Blind Side, The 205
Blonde Snapper 66
bobsled
movies about 210
Bohn, Jason 172
Bojangles Coliseum 19
Bolt, Usain 37, 47–50, 53, 54
Bolton Wanderers 15–16
Borg-Warner Trophy 144
Borzov, Valery 53
bowling
movies about 206
boxing
age in 22
calories burnt 179
injuries in 33
memorabilia 168
movies about 202, 203, 204, 205, 206
Brenkus, John 48
Brentford FC 45
Brighton and Hove Albion 16, 196–7, 198
Brisbane Roar 183
Brooks, Lance 39
Brosch, Al 172
Bundle, Matthew 50–1